The Black Arc

IMAGE OF
THE FENDAHL

By Simon Bucher-Jones

Published in 2016 by Obverse Books

Cover Design © Cody Schell

Text © Simon Bucher-Jones, 2016

Simon would like to thank:

*My editor Philip Purser-Hallard, my publisher Stuart Douglas, my
fellow Black Archivists James Cooray Smith, Andrew Hickey, and
Jonathan Dennis for help and comments on various drafts, and Paul
Castle for help and hard-copies of the research materials I didn't
own and couldn't buy on kindle.*

To my family, Sarah, Morgan, and Rhianna who helped either with comments or with putting up with my watching this **again**.

CONTENTS

OVERVIEW

Serial Title: *Image of the Fendahl*

Writer: Chris Boucher

Director: George Spenton-Foster

Original UK Transmission Dates: 29 October 1977 – 19 November 1977

Running Time:

Episode 1: 24m 38s

Episode 2: 24m 44s

Episode 3: 24m 22s

Episode 4: 20m 32s

UK Viewing Figures: Episode 1: 6.7 million

Episode 2: 7.5 million

Episode 3: 7.9 million

Episode 4: 9.1 million

Regular cast: Tom Baker (The Doctor), Louise Jamieson (Leela)

Guest Cast: Wanda Ventham (Thea Ransome), Daphne Heard (Martha Tyler), Dennis Lill (Dr Fendelman), Edward Evans (Ted Moss), Scott Fredericks (Maximillian Stael), Edward Arthur (Adam Colby), Derek Martin (David Mitchell), Graham Simpson (Hiker), Geoffrey Hinsliff (Jack Tyler)

Antagonists: The Fendahl Core, Max Stael

Novelisation: *Doctor Who and the Image of the Fendahl* by Terrance Dicks. **The Target Doctor Who Library** #34.

Sequels and Prequels: *The Taking of Planet 5* (book, 1999), **Kaldor City** (audio series, 2001-04), *Deus Le Volt* (novella, 2006).

Responses:

'...one of the best stabs at outright horror in **Doctor Who**'s history.'

[Paul Cornell, Martin Day, Keith Topping, *Doctor Who: The Discontinuity Guide*, p216]

'Chris Boucher's third contribution to **Doctor Who** is probably his weakest [and] once more owes a clear debt to the "Daemons" prototype.'

[John Kenneth Muir, *A Critical History of Doctor Who on Television*, p261]

SYNOPSIS

Episode 1

At the Priory, a mansion in the village of Fetchborough, a team of scientists is investigating a groundbreaking discovery. Research by **Dr Fendelman**, an electronics mogul, has led palaeontologist **Adam Colby** to the burial site in Kenya of a human skull, which his colleague **Thea Ransome** has dated to 12 million years before the present, long before *Homo sapiens* is believed to have evolved.

Fendelman and his assistant **Max Stael** are using secret experimental equipment to scan the skull's history from a separate laboratory in the Priory. This appears to create a number of simultaneous effects: Thea becoming mesmerised by the suddenly glowing skull; the mysterious pursuit of a panicked hiker in the nearby woods; and the diversion of the TARDIS in flight. Leaving behind an inoperative K-9, the **Doctor** and **Leela** search the environs of Fetchborough for the source of the 'sonic time scan', which threatens to destroy the Earth. A local, **Ted Moss**, tells them what little he knows of the scientists and their work.

When the Priory team discover the hiker's body, Fendelman insists on concealing it, and calls in a security team from his backers in London. The head of security, **Mitchell**, antagonises the elderly cook **Martha Tyler**, who warns him before she leaves the Priory that he'll regret it. Fendelman, who tells a scornful Colby that his equipment allows him to look into the past, sets off another scan. Thea again becomes entranced, this time in the empty lab.

7

The Doctor is seemingly paralysed in the woods as an unseen antagonist approaches, while Leela is ambushed at a cottage by a hooded figure with a shotgun.

Episode 2

Leela easily overpowers her assailant, the now belligerent Moss, and meets **Jack Tyler**, the grandson of Mrs Tyler whose cottage this is. Jack sends Moss away, believing that he is involving his grandmother, the local wise woman, in some sinister enterprise.

The Doctor manages to escape his assailant, which seemingly kills Mitchell at the Priory. Thea and Colby examine the guard's body, but Thea collapses just as the Doctor arrives. He and Colby see two snakelike creatures the Doctor calls 'embryo Fendahleen', apparently emerging from her inert form.

The increasingly paranoid Fendelman believes that the skull (which in X-rays shows a crude pentagram as part of its bone structure) is evidence of an extraterrestrial origin for humanity. He has the Doctor locked up as a spy, and the phones disconnected before Colby can call the police. Recovering, Thea bizarrely claims to Colby that the whole situation has been planned – by her. She is later drugged by Stael, who leads a local coven of which Moss is a member.

Mrs Tyler arrives home, in a state of terrible shock having seen something monstrous in the woods, and Leela goes to the Priory to find the Doctor. The Doctor escapes in time to be captivated and tormented by the glowing skull.

Episode 3

Leela rescues the Doctor and they return to Mrs Tyler's cottage, where they revive the old woman from her fugue state. They discuss the powers of precognition and telepathy she has gained from growing up near Fetchborough's local time fissure, and her vision of a hungry presence seeking to eat her soul.

Stael ties Thea up in the Priory's cellars, where he has set up a traditional altar and pentagram, claiming that she is a focus of the ancient power of the locale. He forces Fendelman and Colby at gunpoint to join her.

The Doctor takes Leela on an exploratory mission in the TARDIS, asking Jack to watch the Priory in their absence. He tells her that the skull came from the fifth planet of Earth's solar system, and is a relic of **the Fendahl**, a creature from Time Lord mythology that absorbs life and embodies death. They discover that the fifth planet was time-looped by the Time Lords 12 million years previously, but that the skull escaped. It has been affecting humanity's development ever since.

Stael and his coven link the skull to Fendelman's scanning equipment (which unbeknownst to them has nearly reached the threshold to destroy the planet), releasing the power stored in the skull's own pentagram which will allow the Fendahl to manifest itself. Fendelman realises before Stael kills him that not only he, but all his ancestors, have been manipulated to bring about this moment.

Returning to the Priory, the Doctor, Leela and the Tylers are menaced by a fully-grown Fendahleen.

Episode 4

The Doctor kills the Fendahleen with Jack's shotgun, which Martha has loaded with salt — an ancient occult protection against evil. In the cellar, Thea is transformed into the humanoid Fendahl Core, and begins transmuting Moss and the other coven members into Fendahleen. The Doctor and Leela rescue Colby, but are too late to help the immobilised Stael — except by giving him a gun to use on himself.

The Doctor explains that the Fendahl is a gestalt creature, consisting of the Fendahl Core and 12 Fendahleen. There were 12 members of the coven, but with one Fendahleen dead and Stael now unavailable for transmogrification, the Fendahl is incomplete and relatively weak. Armed with more salt from the Priory kitchen, and menaced by Fendahleen and the teleporting Core, the Doctor and his allies succeed in rigging Fendelman's scanner, and stealing the skull from the cellar before it creates a catastrophic explosion, destroying the manifesting Fendahl.

Colby and the Tylers escape to Martha's cottage, while the Doctor and Leela head off in the TARDIS, to drop the skull into a supernova before the Doctor repairs K-9.

CHAPTER 1: AUDIENCE EXPECTATIONS

'A hole in time, a human skull eight million years older than man, strange deaths in the English countryside – a nerve-racking adventure begins for the Doctor and Leela.'[1]

[*Radio Times*]

Nowadays with a whole internet throwing spoilers at us, and website upon website of fannish speculation – as well as actual trailers on television – it's hard to remember (even for those of us who were there) and maybe even harder to imagine (if you weren't), that once upon a time all we had to go on for what **Doctor Who** was going to be like next was a line or two in the *Radio Times* – and what we had been educated to expect by what we'd come to know the programme was doing[2].

Before we get into discussing *Image of the Fendahl* (1977) (hereafter *Image*) then, I'd like to briefly sketch out the likely audience expectations for the story, based on **Doctor Who**'s then-recent history, covering Tom Baker's tenure as the Doctor – and specifically the period 1975-77 as produced by Philip Hinchcliffe, which finished three stories earlier with *The Talons of Weng-Chiang* (1977).

---

[1] *Radio Times*, 29 October to 4 November 1977. Accessed via the BBC Genome Project.

[2] I can still remember the excitement I felt when the *Radio Times Doctor Who Special* for the 10th anniversary (1973) printed an episode guide for the first part of Jon Pertwee's 1974 season before it had aired! I was nine, and this might have been when I realised that **Doctor Who** wasn't just beamed straight from the BBC to our televisions, but had to be constructed first.

From the start of the fourth Doctor's adventures, the stories drew fairly straightforwardly and unashamedly from film and literary sources. His first story, *Robot* (1974-75), adopts the bathos of *King Kong* (1933), with the eponymous giant monster lifting the relatively diminutive Sarah Jane Smith to the top of the bunker. It also uses the 'robot that cannot harm a human without overloading its brain' trope from Isaac Asimov's **Robot** stories, via Robbie the Robot in *Forbidden Planet* (1956).

Baker's second story, *The Ark in Space* (1975) – while predating *Alien* (1979) – has the same similarity as *Alien* to 'Discord in Scarlet', AE van Vogt's second published science fiction (SF) story, in which a creature capable of surviving in space takes humans – travelling in space – as the hosts for its eggs[3]. *The Ark in Space* is actually a more inventive use of the idea than either *Alien* or the earlier 'thing loose on a space-ship' film *It! The Terror From Beyond Space* (1958).

Across its 13th and 14th seasons (Baker's second and third series), **Doctor Who** was gloriously revelling in referencing and playing with horror and SF film tropes. At the most reductionist level, this can be played as a game of 'influence consequences':

---

[3] Published in the December 1939 issue of *Astounding Science-Fiction*, and later incorporated as chapters 13 to 21 of the 'fix-up' novel *The Voyage of The Space Beagle* (1950).

Invasion of the Body Snatchers (1956) (Shape-changing aliens replace our friends)

+   *Gorgo* (1961) (A prehistoric monster comes from Scotland to attack London)[4]

=   *Terror of the Zygons* (1975).

Forbidden Planet (1956) (An invisible force, shown at times as a red-flecked animation, attacks a survey ship coming to a distant world to check on a previous expedition, whose surviving scientist has meddled in things that his culture is not yet ready to master)

+   *Dr Jekyll and Mr Hyde* (1931 et al) (A scientist uses a potion to control his regression to a bestial form)

=   *Planet of Evil* (1975).

The Thing from Another World (1951) (An alien plant that lives off human blood is found at the Pole)

+   *The Quatermass Xperiment* (1955) (A human who comes into contact with something alien grows into a monstrous mass atop a building that has to destroyed for the sake of the world before it spores)

=   *The Seeds of Doom* (1976).

---

[4] Gorgo was the monster in a cheerful British knock-off of the *The Beast From 20,000 Fathoms* (1953) / *Godzilla* (1954) genre, in which the Mama Gorgo – bless – kicks London to bits to rescue its baby which has been captured by scientists and cruelly put in a zoo. At the end they go back to the only home they know. 'They're going back now, back to the sea' intones the smiling Scottish child at the end.

> ***Frankenstein*** (any of them, but mostly the Universal series 1931-48, beginning with one of the best films of all time and ending with Abbott and Costello) (A scientist works out of a castle, has a hunchback assistant – admittedly originally called Fritz – and is menaced by a mob of villagers with torches; his monster's evil is the fault of its having been given the brain of a homicidal madman)
>
> + ***She*** (1965) (An immortal woman whose longevity derives from a mysterious scared flame)
> + ***They Saved Hitler's Brain*** (1968) (What it says on the tin)
> + ***Forbidden Planet*** again (The villain's name)
> = ***The Brain of Morbius*** (1976).

The Pyramids of Mars (1975), *The Hand of Fear* (1976), *The Deadly Assassin* (1976), and *The Talons of Weng-Chiang* (1977) all show similar degrees of influence by or homage to films: Universal's **Mummy** films, *The Beast With Five Fingers* (1946) (an evil disembodied hand), *The Manchurian Candidate* (1962) (an engineered political assassination), and the **Fu Manchu** series beginning with *The Mask of Fu Manchu* (1932) (the trope of the evil Chinese mastermind), respectively.

Now, this is not in any way a criticism of those stories in the sense of reflecting on their quality or even their originality; and the formula certainly wasn't disliked by the wide television audience, for **Doctor Who** was going through one of its periods of both critical and (insofar as the BBC is concerned about such things) commercial and market share success. These, after all, are the stories that are most recalled when people praise the fourth Doctor as one of the series' all-time bests, if not 'the' iconic Doctor[5]. A good story draws on all the things the writer knows or has seen – good images repeat in fiction because they work; good ideas repeat in fiction because they generate a dialogue between the source and the work created in response. I would personally rate many of these stories – perhaps most of them – among the best adventure dramas ever made on British television, but knowing that the previous two years' worth of **Doctor Who** works in this way suggests a prima facie question the audience (and we) might want to ask of *Image of the Fendahl* – namely: 'What delights are you spreading out for us from the great menu of film and fiction, and what are you going to do to entertain us with them?'

Of special interest to us in considering *Image* as latter-day critics (the audience at the time en masse would not have been keeping score of such things, although the fannish minority might already have been) are *The Face of Evil* (1977) and *The Robots of Death* (1977), the earlier stories written for **Doctor Who** by *Image*'s author Chris Boucher.

The Face of Evil may have been influenced by *Zardoz* (1974), in which a future world (in *Zardoz*'s case Earth) is divided between an overly civilised group, which is developing mental powers and another group, which has reverted to a primitive, savage existence and who the first group's (partial) location within a giant stone

---

[5] In 2014, the 50th anniversary poll in *Doctor Who Magazine* (DWM) #474 voted Tom Baker the best Doctor with 21.69% of the vote, and *Genesis of the Daleks, The Talons of Weng-Chiang*, and *Pyramids of Mars* from this period of the show at numbers 3, 6, and 8 respectively out of a total number of 241 then-televised stories.

head is designed to cow and overawe. In *The Face of Evil,* the scary stone face is that of the Doctor – 'the Evil One', according to the Sevateem. Chris Boucher uses the split setting to tell a story of the Doctor's moral responsibility for past actions, of a powerful force worshipped as a god that has its own mad agenda, and of a history that has been forgotten. These themes – the past coming back with consequences that must be faced, however fearful, the inhuman nature of worshipped things, and the fact that the history taught (by faith, in the person of the High Priest Neeva, and science in the form of the beliefs of the Tesh) is a lie – will be revisited in *Image.*

Chris Boucher's second script for **Doctor Who**, *The Robots of Death,* is more recent at the time of *Image,* but less directly parallel to it. It is clearly influenced both by Agatha Christie's 'Someone in this room is a murderer' style of detective fiction (particularly the often-retitled *And Then There Were None* (1939), and *Murder On The Orient Express* (1934), where the victim, the suspects and the investigator are all trapped alone in a vehicle large enough to be an 'environment') and Isaac Asimov's first two **Robot** novels and his short stories collected as *I, Robot* (1950) (the idea that robots would be designed to have inbuilt inhibitory laws against harming humans is his). As well as a bravura piece of worldbuilding and atmosphere (for which much of the credit must rest with set, special effects and costume design), *The Robots of Death* is an extremely effective science fiction mystery. This is a form which before Asimov's *The Caves of Steel* (1954) was considered impossible, and which so famous an SF writer as Larry Niven has professed to find challenging:

> 'A detective story is a puzzle. In principle at least, the reader can know what crime was committed, by whom,

and how and where and why, before the story hits him in the face with it. [...]

'Science fiction is an exercise in imagination [...] Strange backgrounds, odd societies following odd laws, and unfamiliar values and ways of thinking are the rule.

'Now, how can the reader anticipate the detective if all the rules are strange?'[6]

What does this tell us about what we should be expecting from Chris Boucher and from **Doctor Who** as we approach *Image?* Perhaps a story drawing on a fairly well-known film source, that would marry its horrific elements with a knowledge of science fiction and a capacity for world-building, with well-drawn characters and a central mystery? Perhaps a story in which the past is important, and its errors bleed into the present, and the gods are mad.

We can also see in *The Robots of Death* a playful tendency to embed references in the names of characters, a mixture of 'in-jokes' for those in the know about science fiction, and a means of building thematic resonance[7]. This can be intrusive if done badly,

---

[6] Niven, Larry, *Flatlander: The Collected Tales of Gil Hamilton* (1995), p354.
[7] The character of Poul is a nod to science fiction writer Poul Anderson, while the name of the mastermind behind the robots, Taren Kapel, is a reference to Karel Čapek, whose SF play *RUR* (1920) first coined the word 'robot'. (One of *The Robots of Death*'s terms for what we would now call the 'uncanny valley' – a phrase not coined until 1978 – is 'Grimwade's syndrome', which refers to Peter Grimwade, the director of model shots on the serial. While Tom Baker changed the reference from the scripted 'Grimwold's

but I find Chris Boucher's handling of it in *The Robots of Death* (and, as we shall see, in *Image*, where it is foregrounded in a very effective piece of characterisation), to be charming, and not destructive to the suspension of disbelief. The fannish contingent of **Doctor Who** watchers in 1977[8], if they had known that the third story of season 15 was also to be by Chris Boucher, might have expected some interesting wordplay around the characters' names.

We, and they, might also expect a degree of comedy – *The Robots of Death* contains an excellent comic turn from D84, the deadpan robot detective who is disguised as a lower form of robot (a 'Dum') and is consequently not supposed to be able to speak – but is nevertheless capable of being amusingly ironic about it:

> 'This is a communicator. It can function on either human or robot command circuits. Would you like to use it? I cannot speak.'[9]

However, the backstage crew of **Doctor Who** was about to change, and some of these expectations would be impacted by that. Robert Holmes, the Script Editor whose last commission was *Image*, was

---

Syndrome', this is perhaps only a slightly disguised form of the same joke.)

[8] In 1977, the first **Doctor Who** convention in Britain – so far as is known – was held by the Doctor Who Appreciation Society at 'a Church Hall in Battersea' ('Doctor Who Appreciation Society 1977 Convention'). The one-day event had three guests: Jon Pertwee, Tom Baker and Louise Jameson. While of course all of fandom couldn't have attended a church hall, this is, perhaps, a sign that it was not very large. O'Day, Andrew, 'Social Spaces: British Fandom to the Present', in Leitch, Gillian I, *Doctor Who in Time and Space*, pp25-43.

[9] *The Robots of Death,* episode 3.

about to leave, and Philip Hinchcliffe, the show's Producer, had left after *The Talons of Weng-Chiang*. *Image* would be produced by Graham Williams and script-edited (into its final form) by Anthony Read. Such changes of personnel occur regularly over the long history of **Doctor Who**, but this one coincided with, or was caused by, exterior pressures that would begin to change the tone of the show.

The Wider TV Landscape: Issues with Horror in 1977

One possible view of *Image of the Fendahl* is that it's the last of the great Gothic **Doctor Who** stories, coming after the thoroughly Gothed-up season 14 run from *The Masque of Mandragora* (1976) to *The Talons of Weng-Chiang*, and the first two season 15 stories *Horror of Fang Rock* and *The Invisible Enemy* (both 1977) – the latter of which begins the move away from Gothic, referencing a more family-friendly SF film, *Fantastic Voyage* (1956), and introducing the child-pleasing icon K-9 to the show. Another is that *Image* is part of a pale version of those more full-bloodedly Gothic works, as the BBC caved into minority public opinion.

The former view is espoused by Alan Barnes when he refers to Image as 'the last acknowledged gasp of the Gothic Group', and the latter also – perhaps – when he goes on to say of the Amicus films he mentions in passing: 'If you like these, you'll love *Image of the Fendahl*, heaven help you'[10].

The latter view is directly stated by Patrick Mulkern:

---

[10] Barnes, Alan, 'The Fact of Fiction: Image of the Fendahl', DWM #379.

> '*Image of the Fendahl* is often cited as the last gasp of the horror sub-genre prevalent in earlier seasons. But punches are pulled. The hiker's decomposing corpse isn't shown, and both Fendelman's murder and Stael's suicide occur off camera.'[11]

Barnes rejects as a myth, however, the argument that 'the horror-tinged tales of the first few Tom Baker years owed their style and content to the Hammer Film back catalogue,' calling the assertion 'rubbish' because Hammer films 'reinforce superstition'[12].

Barnes is, I believe, wrong to dismiss the influence of the **style** of Hammer on the 'Gothic Group'; and because he has focused on the Gothic strand of Hammer films alone as an influence, and neglected the parallel post-Gothic strand derived from Nigel Kneale, I believe he is also wrong to reject its influence on **content**. Mulkern, while right to note a reduction in obvious grue, is wrong to assert that this amounts to deflating the horror of the story. Rather, I would contend, *Image* functions in a way which works past these 'gothic' events to a terror that transcends them, by melding the grounded unease of Kneale with the mists and witchcraft of the Gothic.

Before we get to a detailed analysis of those influences, however, we need to look at why, by season 15, they were waning – and what effect that passing would have on *Image*.

---

[11] Mulkern, Patrick, 'Doctor Who Story Guide: Image of the Fendahl'.
[12] Barnes, 'The Fact of Fiction'.

The Mary Whitehouse Effect

Constance Mary Whitehouse CBE, first president and founder of the National Viewers and Listener's Association (founded in 1965, known since 2001 as Mediawatch-UK), was running a campaign against – among other things – permissiveness, liberalism, sex and violence on television. Irrespective of whether or not her views were justified, it is certain that by the mid to late 70s she had set her sights on **Doctor Who**. The period in which Philip Hinchcliffe produced the series (beginning in 1975 with *The Ark In Space* and ending in 1977 with *The Talons of Weng-Chiang*) drew the majority of her complaints, and some fan commentators have suggested that the handover to the new Producer Graham Williams (*Image of the Fendahl* being his third story in this capacity, although it would have been commissioned under Hinchcliffe[13]) may have been influenced by her complaints to the BBC.

Hinchcliffe himself says that he was happy to leave, that it had been 'three heavy years' and that he was 'rostered off' (that is, moved by the organization, on a rota of producers) to take over a new police show, **Target** (1977-78). As a producer under contract to the BBC at that time, he could be moved between shows in this way, and indeed he has stated he preferred the system to freelancing in many ways because it allowed for paid 'developmental' time between assignments. Ironically he states that he was later 'accused by the Director General' of making the first series of **Target** 'a bit rather [sic] violent and brutish', and he

---

[13] Stevens, Alan, 'Image of the Fendahl'.

was to move on to work on **Shoestring** (1979-80) with Robert Banks Stewart, and thereafter to freelance work[14].

Some examples of Whitehouse's concerns about **Doctor Who** were:

- *The Brain of Morbius*: 'perhaps I can recount the [...] call from the mother of a boy of six [who] woke up screaming every night.'[15]
- Philip Hinchcliffe's team creating 'some of the sickest and most horrific material ever seen on children's television,' having 'an obsession with manic atrocities [...] inoculated by the very excesses of their own imagination.'[16]
- A cut-out Leela figure included in the *Radio Times* for a 'Blue Peter Dr Who Toy Theatre' having a 'rather lethal knife'.[17]
- *Seeds of Doom*: 'Strangulation – by hand, by claw, by obscene vegetable matter – is the latest gimmick, sufficiently close up so they get the point. And just for a little variety, show the children how to make a Molotov Cocktail.'[18]

---

[14] Interviewed in 'Life After Who – Philip Hinchcliffe', *The Android Invasion* DVD release (2012).

[15] Thompson Ben, *Ban This Filth! Letters from the Mary Whitehouse Archive* (2012) p251.

[16] Thompson, *Ban This Filth!* p251.

[17] Thompson, *Ban This Filth!* p252. The phrase occurs in Michael Swann's response which is quoted, but he is clearly echoing her complaint.

[18] Thompson, *Ban This Filth!* p251.

Whitehouse's concerns about *The Deadly Assassin* prompted an apology from the then Director-General, Sir Charles Curran. The focus of her concern was a freeze-frame cliffhanger ending to episode 3 in which the Doctor appeared to drown. According to John Tulloch and Manuel Alvarado, the result of this was a direct move from 'horror' under Hinchcliffe to 'comedy' under Williams:

> 'The turn to comedy was "entirely, directly" related to the Whitehouse attack. "It was replacing the violence... that was a very, very major part of the thinking." Hence Williams' new signature of "suspense following light relief" was established, "because in a thriller situation, if you can't have the nasties, it's a vacuum..."'[19]

Season 15 therefore begins with stories with horrific elements, commissioned under Philip Hinchcliffe and Robert Holmes, being produced by their successors. Graham Williams is on record as saying that having to remove the horror, his inclination was to lighten the tone and to add comedy, but also that he was directly instructed to do so:

> 'I was at this point being offered the job but with an absolutely clear dictate – it was a brief, it was a dictate – that the violence level had to come down, and the horror element with it! The moment I protested that this was what the audience for 'Doctor Who' adored, I was shouted down.'[20]

---

[19] Tulloch, John, and Manuel Alvarado, *Doctor Who: The Unfolding Text*, pp158-159.
[20] 'Graham Williams (1980s)'.

Image of the Fendahl: A Post-Gothic Horror?

I think, and hope to persuade you, that although *Image* is profoundly influenced by the Gothic, both within and outside **Doctor Who**, it is in fact **neither** a last hurrah of that form (which, irrespective of the influence of Mary Whitehouse on television, had already begun to be played out in the cinema in 1968 with the release of *Rosemary's Baby* and its negative effects on the success of Hammer Film Productions), **nor** a vitiated pastiche of that form resulting from Whitehouse's criticisms of the BBC's production of **Doctor Who**.

Image is a modernist development from the Gothic that stands as a different sort of horror in its own right, which – had she understood what it was actually saying – should have appalled Whitehouse far more than a cardboard cut-out figure's cardboard knife. It should be judged in post-Gothic terms, and in those terms it works superbly well. (This is not to say it's without flaws, but I intend to look at these later.) It's also very funny – in a way that works with the grain of the characterization and enhances the drama – and a third way of looking at it would be in the light of that very difficult form, the horror-comedy.

It is a work that is influenced by many different sources: not just by Hammer films or their Gothic literature roots, but by films made by Hammer's single largest competitor, Amicus, and by other texts including (as we will see) the works of Nigel Kneale, HP Lovecraft, Arthur C Clarke[21] and the astronomers of the 19th century.

---

[21] At one point Fendelman – who's obviously read Clarke's short story 'The Sentinel' (1951) or seen *2001 : A Space Odyssey* (1968) – suggests that the Skull might send a signal to aliens when scanned

Image, like its successor **Doctor Who** stories *The Sun Makers* (1977), *Underworld* (1978) and *The Invasion of Time* (1978), is a reaction away from the Gothic model which dominated the Hinchcliffe years. Each of these diverges further still – into political satire, a retelling of Greek myth, and the show's own mythology – until by *The Invasion of Time*, very little of the Gothic remains[22]; but *Image,* unlike the remaining stories of season 15, retains enough of the Gothic mode to function both as a divergence from, and a critique of, it.

---

with sufficiently high technology, acting as a beacon to show that intelligent life is established on Earth. (In the short story a pyramid, and in the film, the famous black monolith, both on the Moon, serve this purpose.) Ah, if only it were that benign.

[22] The Gothic has been exiled from **Doctor Who** at this point just as the Outsiders have been removed from the Citadel of the Time Lords.

CHAPTER 2: THE INFLUENCE OF GOTHIC HORROR

'What part does witchcraft play in the events around the old priory? And what are the strange creatures which materialise from Thea? Only the Doctor realises their dangerous significance.'[23]

[*Radio Times*]

Witchcraft – check; an old priory – check; strange materialisations – check! This sounds like Gothic, but what **exactly** do we mean by the term? In this context we're referring to the mode of the Gothic novel, and the films that later echo it.

Like all literary terms, 'Gothic' covers a continuum of approaches and themes, and to some extent (like, famously, science fiction) it could be defined as 'what we point at when we say it' – but in its origin, the Gothic was a fashionable form of popular literature beginning in English with Horace Walpole's *The Castle of Otranto: A Gothic Story* (1764). This form grew from Germanic folk tales and ghost stories brought back from the Black Forest by returnees from the 'Grand Tour', and is characterised by 'the macabre, the fantastic, and supernatural, usually set amid haunted castle, graveyards, ruins and wild picturesque landscapes.'[24] A more recent, less formulaic definition is: 'A mode of narrative fiction dealing with supernatural or horrifying events, and generally possessed of a claustrophobic air of oppression or evil', although

---

[23] *Radio Times*, 5 to 11 November 1977.
[24] Drabble, Margaret, ed, *The Oxford Companion to English Literature* (fifth edition, 1995), p411.

this might be criticised as reading like a definition of all horrific narrative prose[25].

The form takes 'Gothic' as its descriptive title by analogy with the western European architectural style of the 12th to 16th centuries: the high pointed arches, rib vaults, and flying buttresses, with stone tracery, which we would associate with medieval priories and castles. Gothic is a sort of darkly romantic fairy tale – in which there may well be no happy endings, or the happiness may be the happiness of the monsters. Famous Gothic works which were widely circulated in England, often in French translated from the German, and which would have been read by Mary and Percy Shelley, Lord Byron and Dr Polidori (among others) included the five-volume *Gespensterbuch* (1811-15) jointly edited by Friedrich Schulze and the playwright Johann Apel, which contained the stories Mary Shelley cited as influences upon *Frankenstein* (first edition 1818, revised edition 1831)[26].

It is no coincidence that the seven Gothic narratives mentioned by Jane Austen in her parody of the Gothic, *Northanger Abbey* (1818), were either first published in German or sound as if they should

---

[25] Birch, Dinah, ed, *The Oxford Companion to English Literature* (seventh Edition, 2009) p430.

[26] Shelley, Mary, 'Some German Stories of Ghosts', in *Frankenstein* (Oxford World's Classics 1818 text), p4. The stories are listed in the explanatory notes (p253) as the French translation by Jean Baptiste Benoit Eyres, of the *Gespensterbuch*. In French its title was the resounding *Fantasmagoria, ou Recuil d'Histoires d'Apparitions des Spectres, Revents, Fantomes, etc, traduit de l'Allemand, par un Amateur* (1812). Their origin in the German is set out in the introduction to an English reprint: Hale, Terry, ed, *Tales of the Dead: Ghost Stories of the Villa Diodati* (1992).

have been[27]. Nowadays we tend to think of *Frankenstein* as a Gothic novel, but this is because of the way the book has been presented on film – castles, lightning, a hunchbacked assistant, machinery – which in retrospect resembles the excesses of steampunk more than the actual realisation of the descriptions in the book.

John Sutherland, Lord Northcliffe Professor of English Literature at University College London, points out that this techno-Gothic methodology of Frankenstein's birth is 'wholly unfaithful to what Mary Shelley wrote in 1818.'[28] Taking this as a cue, I would argue that *Frankenstein* **begins** the post-Gothic, in which science is shone into things that were considered the domain of God (or the Devil) in the Gothic proper, and which – while it results in horror for the characters, and is expressed in a horrific way – is concerned not with what lurks in the unexplored darkness of the forest, but with the consequences of what we discover in the glare of the 'Age of Enlightenment' already under way.

As we will see, it would only be a marginal overstatement to characterise the Gothic as Horror, and the Post-Gothic as Science Fiction. This view is shared by Brian Aldiss, who cites *Frankenstein* as the first science fiction novel in his study of the genre, and Mary

---

[27] They are *The Necromancer: Or The Tale of the Black Forest* (1794) by Ludwig Flammenberg, *Horrid Mysteries* (1796) by the Marquis de Grosse, *The Midnight Bell* (1798) by Francis Lathom, *Castle of Wolfenbach* (1793) by Eliza Parsons, *The Mysterious Warning: A German Tale* (1796) by Eliza Parsons, *Clermont* (1798) by Regina Maria Roche, and *The Orphans of the Rhine: A Romance* (1798) by Eleanor Sleath. Austen, Jane, *Northanger Abbey*. Wordsworth Classics edition, p21.

[28] Sutherland, John, *Is Heathcliff a Murderer?* (1996), p24.

Shelley as the Mother of Science Fiction[29]. Alan Moore suggests that:

> 'All Horror – or most Horror up to Lovecraft – had all been predicated on the Gothic tradition, which is a tradition where you have an enormous vertical weight in time that is bearing down upon a fragile present. A history of dark things in the past that are bleeding up to some terrifying denouement in the present day.'[30]

It is the intertwining of the Post-Gothic – that is, of Lovecraftian horror, of science fiction horror, of modern horror – with the Gothic that produces the strangeness of effect in *Image*.

The Gothic in English prose runs from the 1760s to 1797[31] at its height as 'literature', and gets a revival in the poetry of the Romantics around 1818-1819, but it continues into the 19th century increasingly in narratives aimed at the popular end of the market such as *Varney the Vampire* (1845-47) and *Wagner, the Wehr-Wolf* (1846-47) (sadly *Gerty the Ghoul* has been lost to us[32]). More 'serious' literary exploration of its themes is handled by parodies such as *Northanger Abbey* (1818, though written c1799), and Thomas Love Peacock's *Nightmare Abbey* (1818), and the growth of specialised forms, such as the Victorian ghost story that reaches a crystalline expression in the works of MR James.

---

[29] Aldiss, Brian, *Trillion Year Spree*, pp19, 48.

[30] Doctorow, Cory, 'Alan Moore on Lovecraft and the 20th Century'.

[31] From Walpole's *The Castle of Otranto* (1764) to Anne Radcliffe's last novel *The Italian* (1797).

[32] A joke – don't look for this. (On the other hand I would write it for money.)

There is a reason the first volume of James' fiction is *Ghost Stories of an Antiquary* (1904): ghosts (except in **Doctor Who**, where it's 50-50 that they might be from the future) are **necessarily** things of the past. The Gothic form is now in essence retrogressive (as it was even as early as *The Castle of Otranto*[33]): it hankers back to a previous non-industrialised age in which the threats are supernatural and can be defused by placing your faith wholly and unquestioningly in the God of your fathers (or mothers). The Gothic admits of no need for explanations. Its effects are drawn broadly and with startling violence upon a grand and awesome canvas which begins in the Black Forest, and is bounded by the arabesques of William Beckford's *Vathek* (1786) to the East, and the Antarctic of Arthur Gordon Pym (in Edgar Allan Poe's *The Narrative of Arthur Gordon Pym of Nantucket* (1838)) to the South. Of the West (and the New World) it says little. Bram Stoker's *Dracula* (1897) is Gothic (more so than *Frankenstein*); Samuel Coleridge's *The Rime of the Ancient Mariner* (1798) is Gothic. In America, Poe's horrors are Gothic about half the time (his detective and science fiction narratives falling in a different mode); and the first horror films which begin in a German expressionism steeped in the same dark romantic tradition (*The Cabinet of Dr Caligari* (1920), *Nosferatu*

---

[33] While Walpole writes in his 'Preface to the Second Edition' that *Otranto* was 'an attempt to blend the two kinds of romance, the ancient and the modern' (p21), the 'modern' he means is a characterisation modelled after the degree of psychological accuracy found in, to use his own example, Shakespeare. *Otranto* is not 'modern' in any substantive sense at the level of plot.

(1922) etc) are Gothic. The **Gormenghast** novels of Meryvn Peake are staggeringly Gothic[34].

In the 1960s and 1970s, though, the greatest and most popular form of Gothic fiction in the UK wasn't old books, but the lurid technicolour of film, particularly the films made by Hammer Productions – now generally known under the title of 'Hammer Horror'.

The Influence of Hammer Horror

When we think now of Hammer films we think almost entirely of the sequence that began in 1955, maybe even those beginning with their first colour horror feature *The Curse of Frankenstein* (1957), but Hammer as a commercial entity dates back to 1934. From 1934 to 1955 the studio made a great number of films, either thrillers in a hard-boiled American style or based on BBC shows such as **The Adventures of PC 49** (1947-53). Before *The Quatermass Xperiment* and *The Curse of Frankenstein* their most commercially successful film was *Family Affair* (1954) – based on **Hi Gang!** (1940-49), the wartime radio broadcasts of Ben Lyons and Bebe Daniels, which would lead in turn to a further BBC radio series, **Life with the Lyons**.

It was not until 1955 that a film based on Nigel Kneale's BBC television serial **The Quatermass Experiment** (1953) would make a still larger profit (the film being imaginatively, or not, retitled *The Quatermass Xperiment* in the UK, to emphasise the horror implicit

---

[34] Peake, Mervyn, *Titus Groan* (1946), *Gormenghast* (1950), *Titus Alone* (1959).

in the relatively new 'X' rating for films [35], and *The Creeping Unknown* in the USA, where 'Quatermass' was not a name that would register with the audience). It set the company off on a track of horror films that were to be big money spinners and come to dominate the company's output.

The Modern

From (almost) the beginning there were two separate threads running through the 'Hammer Horror' films. One thread was the one we've just seen the start of: science fiction 'modern' horror, its tone set by the original BBC **Quatermass** serials and the other plays of Nigel Kneale, and by director Val Guest's insistence that the first **Quatermass** film should be shot as much as possible in a realistic documentary style:

> 'I was very loath to do it. I didn't think it was my cup of tea at all [...] I said I would do it, provided that I could shoot it as if some newsreel company had said, "Go out and cover this story."'[36]

This strand runs as follows:

- *The Quatermass Xperiment* (1955), dir Val Guest. US title *The Creeping Unknown*. Based on Kneale's **The Quatermass Experiment**. Likeliest influences on

---

[35] The 'X' rating replaced 1932's 'H' ('Horrific') rating in the UK in 1951. Until 1970 it meant a film was suitable for viewers aged 16 or over, then until 1982, 18 or over. It was replaced in 1982 by the '18' rating.

[36] Johnson, Tom, *Hammer Films: An Exhaustive Filmography* (Kindle edition) location 2020.

1970s **Doctor Who** – Noah's arm in *The Ark in Space*, the mature Krynoid in *Seeds of Doom*.

- *X the Unknown* (1956), dir Leslie Norman. Original story by Jimmy Sangster (his first screenplay, although he would later write many hits for Hammer) – written 'in house' for want of other **Quatermass**-like material. A radiation-eating life-form from inside the Earth rises to devour nuclear material. Likely influence on **Doctor Who** – the mysterious unexplained forces in *Inferno*.
- *Quatermass 2* (1957), dir Val Guest. US title *Enemy from Space*. Based on Kneale's **Quatermass II** (1955). Likely influence on **Doctor Who** – *Spearhead from Space*.
- *The Abominable Snowman* (1957), dir Val Guest. Based on Kneale's TV play *The Creature* (1955). Likely influence on **Doctor Who** – *The Abominable Snowmen*.

Eventually – I would contend – this strand resurfaces in latter days with the genre of 'shaky-cam', 'handheld' and 'found-footage' horror, of which *Mr Jones* (2013) is perhaps the best recent example, and which has continued to influence **Doctor Who** as recently as *Sleep No More* (2015).

Hammer Films itself (the brand having changed hands several times) began production again with the webcast series **Beyond the Rave** (2008) and has recently produced a work very similar in tone to this strand's **Quatermass** roots in *The Quiet Ones* (2014) – a excellent atmospheric horror about a scientific study of possession.

The works from this strand that are most influential on *Image of the Fendahl* appear to be *Quatermass and the Pit* (1967)[37], and a television work that did not make the transformation to Hammer film, *The Stone Tape* (1972). Both were written by Nigel Kneale.

The Gothic

The second strand of horror in Hammer films begins with *The Curse of Frankenstein*. The screenplay by Jimmy Sangster is a staggering step up in quality from his first screenplay for *X: the Unknown*, but then he was working here with Mary Shelley's *Frankenstein* as a basis rather than attempting a **Quatermass** pastiche. The film sees the first appearance in 'Hammer Horror' of the best-known long-running house director, Terrance Fisher.

Whereas the science-fiction/modern/documentary style of horror is essentially post-Gothic, the intent with *The Curse of Frankenstein* was explicitly to go all-out for the lush Romantic Gothic style. Hammer supremo James Carreras told the *ABC Film Review*: 'We'll give them a classic horror picture – a real good, juicy Gothic thriller.'[38] The key word there is 'juicy' – film Gothic is all about the atmosphere, the tactility of terror, the pith of forbidden fruit.

It is this second strand that really comes to dominate the box office for Hammer, with *Curse* making a profit that in today's terms would equate to £172 million[39]. Given that success it is hardly surprising

---

[37] However, Lance Parkin reports that Chris Boucher denies this (Parkin, Lance, 'The Quatermass Irrelevancy', *Matrix* #51).

[38] Johnson, Tom, *Hammer Films*, location 2290.

[39] The film made £8 million, which was nearly 30 times its cost. £1 in 1957 = £22.35 today (Browning, Richard, 'Historic Inflation Calculator').

that Hammer films increasingly followed this model, with a further series of **Frankenstein** films starring Peter Cushing as Baron Frankenstein, and a **Dracula** series with Christopher Lee as the eponymous Count, as well as films covering other creatures: *The Reptile* (1966), *The Gorgon* (1964), *The Mummy* (1959), the Werewolf (*The Curse of the Werewolf*, 1961), etc, etc.

Building the *Image*: Direct Influences?

These films would have been seen by many young men growing up in the 60s, and Chris Boucher (born in 1943) was of an age to be influenced by them.

The largest influence of any single Hammer film on *Image* is probably *Quatermass and the Pit* (US title *Five Million Years To Earth*), Hammer's version of Nigel Kneale's BBC serial **Quatermass and the Pit** (1958-59). In *Quatermass and the Pit*, relics of aliens from Mars who experimented upon humanity's ancestors are found during excavations in London, together with the skulls of 'ape-men'. A machine is used to access the human race memory and show images of the past, and the psychic or telekinetic power of the Martians is stored within the fabric of their ship – which uses that power to re-emphasise characteristics of hatred and a desire to destroy the unalike that the Martians have engineered into humanity to preserve their culture of hive purges.

A secondary influence would be Kneale's *The Stone Tape*, broadcast on BBC2 in 1972, in which a seemingly supernatural event – a haunting – is subject to scientific scrutiny:

EDDIE

Analyse a spook?

> They once had a go at it with bell, book and candle. Well we are better equipped. Everything we get, Jill's going to programme on the computer.[40]

A wealthy businessman and a team of scientists attempt to make a scientific discovery about the supernatural, by investigating recordings made in the stone of a building: records that play back as ghosts only visible to some. In the process, they awaken a horror that is a much degraded recording made thousands of years before.

As well as the possible influence of the plots of *The Quatermass Xperiment* and *The Stone Tape*, there is also the indirect effect of Hammer's leading ladies. The iconography of Thea Ransome as the Fendahl Core – the diaphanous robes (though moderated by a BBC One tea-time schedule), the pentagram, and the sacrifice – is a distillation of the victims of many a fiend – perhaps most specifically Tanith Carlisle (Nike Arrighi) in *The Devil Rides Out* (1968), who is nearly sacrificed by a devil-worshipping cult in an attempt to summon the Angel of Death – though dressed in the greco-roman robes of *She*.

The Influence of Amicus

While most people thinking about Gothic works in film media in the years running up to *Image* will have focused on Hammer Horror, there has already been some criticism pointing to Hammer's main rival, Amicus Productions, as a direct influence on *Image*. Amicus was founded by Milton Subotsky (known to **Doctor Who** fans for Amicus' production of the two Peter Cushing films, *Dr Who and the*

---

[40] Quoted in *Radio Times*, 29 September to 5 October 1973.

Daleks (1965), and *Daleks: Invasion Earth 2150 AD* (1966)), and Max Roenburg. Its first film was *It's Trad, Dad!* (1962)[41]. In 1965 it began to release what would be a very successful series of portmanteau films, each an anthology of horror tales surrounded by an overarching narrative, most usually of supernatural revenge. The first of these was *Dr Terror's House of Horrors* (1965).

In *Doctor Who: The Discontinuity Guide* (1995), Paul Cornell, Martin Day and Keith Topping cite *Dr Terror's House of Horror* as a source from which Mother Tyler's use of tarot cards in *Image* is drawn[42]. Although it is interesting, by itself this is not a certain identification, as the tarot card reading in *Live and Let Die* (1973) might have been as strong an influence, and Tarot cards are not in themselves so unusual as to necessarily imply a prompting from anything but the author's own creativity.

However, the first non-portmanteau horror film from Amicus is a much more significant source of possible imagery for *Image,* and indeed functions as a prototype of what *Image* would have been without its post-Gothic science-horror elements. Given that Amicus Productions' *The Skull* (1965) is much closer to *Image* than the use of Tarot in *Image* is to its use in *Dr Terror's House of Horror*, I submit that *The Skull*, though not now as well-known as the films referenced by the other stories in **Doctor Who**'s Gothic period (1975-1977), **is** a substantial source for the imagery and some of the basic narrative of the through-plot in *Image*. Alan Barnes

---

[41] Which sounds suspiciously like the source for the film *Keep Your Hair On, Daddio!* in Harry Enfield's satirical look at old films, *Norbert Smith: A Life* (1989).

[42] Cornell, Paul, Martin Day and Keith Topping, *Doctor Who: The Discontinuity Guide*, p214.

mentions it only in passing with other Amicus titles[43] – but can be forgiven as the film has only recently been made widely available on Blu-ray, and received few repeats on British television[44].

The Plot and Imagery of Amicus's *The Skull*

> 'In this vivid and highly imaginative British horror film, Professor Christopher Maitland and Sir Matthew Phillips foolishly attempt to probe the skull's demonic secrets.'[45]
>
> [*Radio Times*]

In *The Skull*, a Skull (surprise, surprise) which at certain times glows with an eerie light, brings madness and death to a professor (Maitland, played by Peter Cushing). The Professor is warned by a colleague (Phillips, played by Christopher Lee) that he 'sincerely believe[s] the skull to be dangerous'. Further, it is the skull of a person who, while not mad, in Sir Matthew's view was 'possessed by an evil spirit, a spirit that still inhabits the skull.' The skull surrounds itself with (or is surrounded by) a cult which is determined to worship it, and which (possibly to save production costs) is both inhuman and unseen: 'Those who use its power [are] invisible beings, spirits from a strange evil world.'

Under its influence, its owners, firstly Sir Matthew and latterly Professor Maitland, are driven to acts they can neither understand nor control. Sir Matthew wastes his fortune buying statues of demons which the skull needs for some unexplained purpose, and

---

[43] Barnes, 'The Fact of Fiction'.

[44] The BBC Genome Project reports three showings, in 1980, 1984, and 1986 respectively.

[45] *Radio Times*, 6 to 12 October 1984.

to possess it Maitland first kills the landlord of the man who tried to sell him the skull which has been stolen from Sir Matthew, and thereafter Sir Matthew himself, and is almost driven to murder his wife. Early in the film Matthew warns Maitland to 'Keep away from the skull.'

Photographed so that lights shine on it, fading in and out to appear as a glow from within, the Skull levitates, throws itself through the glass of a locked cabinet, and reappears in a pentagram that no one seems to have drawn (and which seems to focus rather than impede its power). It forces Maitland to steal the last of the four statues which it had earlier forced Phillips to buy: one which depicts a violent devil, implicitly part of a ritual working of black magic. The film ends with Maitland dead – and the skull back in its pentagram, quietly glowing as it seemingly dreams of its next victim.

The following elements are common, then, to both *The Skull* and *Image of the Fendahl*: an initially unnamed power that is presently held within a skull, which can possess people and drive them to kill, around which strange cults of worship spring up towards an unknown end, and which is associated with pentagrams which do not imprison or control it, but provide it with a supportive halo of evil. Both the DVD covers for *The Skull* and *Image* include illustrations of the Skull and the pentagram.

There are of course, differences. The skull in *The Skull* is that of the infamous Marquis De Sade, who the film stresses was not mad but possessed, implicitly shunting the invention of Sadism off the shoulders of a mortal Marquis – who before possession might have been quite a nice chap, 'a handsome young man when he joined his cavalry regiment, pale, delicate, who looked like an angel' – onto the shoulders of an unnamed evil power[46] (although admittedly it's possible that de Sade invited possession tacitly or deliberately by being such a rotter, despite his appearance). Tellingly, the film critic and author Kim Newman remarks that 'the film would play no differently if the skull was that of Gilles de Rais, or Jack the Ripper'[47] ...or even (we might add) of a nameless hominid of millions of years ago.

---

[46] This ambiguity is driven by Milton Subotsky's desire to be more highbrow than Hammer – which places him in the awkward position of making a film about the Skull of the Marquis de Sade that doesn't ever spell out what de Sade's supposed to have done, and which avoids even a vision of an orgy – electing instead to include a brilliantly weird and very effectively Kafkaesque dream trial scene. In the original short story (which doesn't pull its punches and leaves no ambiguity), this speech ends '...whose foppish diffidence cloaked a strange perversity' (Bloch, Robert, 'The Skull of the Marquis de Sade', p49). The film works better for the ambiguity.

[47] Interview with Kim Newman on *The Skull* Blu-Ray release (2015).

CHAPTER 3: THE ASCENT OF THE FENDAHL – PALAEOARCHAEOLOGY

'The dark forces take control in the old priory. But time is running out for everyone as the Fendahl gathers its power.'[48]

[*Radio Times*]

Image of the Fendahl begins with a blond young man talking to a skull. But this isn't Hamlet and the Skull isn't, at least to begin with, a reminder of all humanity's mortality. Adam Colby jokes about it and calls it 'Eustace', and as an archaeologist he doesn't find it in any way sinister, merely puzzling. Expository dialogue between Colby and his colleague Thea Ransome explains that the skull is anomalously 12 million years old, although still that of 'modern' *Homo sapiens*.

A few years earlier, a story like this might have opened as Terrance Dicks' novelisation does, with the scene of the unnamed hiker being followed through the misty woods at night by an unseen inescapable evil. Such an opening scene would have emphasised horror and danger from the first, and had been a common starting trope in such varied **Doctor Who** stories as *The Dæmons* (1971) (a man in killed in a lonely graveyard by a horrific unseen thing), *The Android Invasion* (a man dressed as a soldier who seems to have suffered an awful trauma walks, a broken man, through a woodland to his seeming death) and, well, many others[49]. The

---

[48] *Radio Times*, 12 to 18 November 1977.
[49] Most recently before *Image* in *The Hand of Fear*, *The Deadly Assassin* and *The Face of Evil* – though in this last, Boucher's first

decision instead to open with Colby's banter marks a shift in emphasis from the supernatural to the scientific, from the Gothic to the post-Gothic, and perhaps, as per Graham Williams' instructions, from 'horror' to 'humour'.

The television serial starts with a demystification of mankind's origins and develops as a post-Gothic narrative in which Gothic elements nevertheless exist. The novelisation, *Doctor Who and the Image of the Fendahl* (1979), begins by contrast as a Gothic, with a dark-haired hiker quoting Coleridge to himself in a misty wood[50]:

'Like one, that on a lonely road,
Doth walk in fear and dread,
And having once turn'd round, walks on
And turns no more his head,
Because he knows, a frightful fiend,

---

story, the death happens off-screen and is only heard. In his second, *The Robots of Death,* no one actually dies until 8m34s, with the scene 1 'violent' moment being a story of a robot masseur that tore someone's arm off. *The Talons of Weng-Chiang*, *The Invisible Enemy* and *The Horror of Fang Rock* similarly avoid violence in their opening scenes. Although public reaction (including that of Mary Whitehouse) to *The Deadly Assassin* cannot have influenced scripts written and filmed before its showing, there does seem to have been a retreat from the 'violent opening death' approach to scene 1 which begins with Chris Boucher's work.

[50] Brian Aldiss links Coleridge with **Doctor Who** in his closing speech for Frankenstein Day at the Bodleian Library (Oxford, 7 October 2008, 'Brian W Aldiss on "Frankenstein"').

'To see and to hear Samuel Taylor belting out "The Ancient Mariner" might not have been to everyone's taste – a bit like early **Doctor Who** – but it is something to have a living poet rampant in the parlour.'

Doth close behind him tread.'[51]

The Rime of the Ancient Mariner by Samuel Taylor Coleridge is recalled by the doomed hiker at the very beginning[52]. It summarises very well the effect, both of the titular monster within the story – which in its Fendahleen form can produce an awful paralysis, as of terror, in its victims as it creeps and crawls and writhes ever so slowly after them – and of the story itself.

Both on television and as a book, *Image* is a superlatively creepy story – it creeps you out (and I'd argue that if it doesn't, you haven't yet understood everything it's saying and doing). Indeed, I shall show that it is, implicitly, the scariest **Doctor Who** story, and I mean that literally – for its terror lies in its implications.

The implications are laid out swiftly and with precision, from the first. The skull has been found by Adam Colby – an archaeologist – in ancient volcanic strata – its age confirmed by his colleague, Thea Ransome, via Potassium-Argon dating. This is a real scientific technique (written as K-Ar dating) based on the rate at which isotopic radioactive potassium (K) changes to argon (Ar). It dates mineral formations (unlike carbon dating which dates the decay of radioactive carbon in dead tissue), for once rock has crystallised the argon can no longer be lost to the atmosphere. (Interestingly, it was used in 2013 by the Mars Curiosity Rover to date rocks on Mars.) Some critics consider the exposition here 'clunky', and have

---

[51] Coleridge, Samuel Taylor, *The Rime of the Ancient Mariner* (1798) lines 451-56. This is the full quotation, which Terrance Dicks elides as part of the hiker's characterisation (see Appendix 1, 'Afterimage of the Fendahl').
[52] Dicks, Terrance, *Doctor Who and the Image of the Fendahl* (1979), p7.

attributed it the Anthony Read's script-editing, but it seems more likely to me that this justification for the investigators' certainty as to the age of the Skull – a crucial part of establishing believability – would have been there from the outset, and hence I would place it, good or bad, at Chris Boucher's door. (I think it works well, and I would contend it is not clunky but naturalistic).

The kiss Adam plants on Thea's hand – while making it clear that he respects her academic prowess, and also finds her attractive – plays nicely into a friendly potential romance (or mock romance) between the characters, one in which the audience is inclined to think Adam rather keener than Thea. According to the DVD documentary, this business was added by the actors, who were left by the director to determine the degree of their characters' involvement, if any. Like the also-unscripted kiss on the check Leela gives Adam as she leaves (knowing she may not see him again – as indeed she doesn't, though not because either of them dies), it adds to the perceived depth of character in the story and helps ground the drama which develops as something affecting real people.

The names of the characters bear some inspection at this point, and 'Thea Ransome' is a very suggestive one. We've seen in *The Robots of Death* that Chris Boucher isn't above embedding an in-joke about SF in a name that is also a clue to a character's role. There is a relatively famous work of science fiction that begins with a man named Ransom hiking through a wood and about to stumble onto a professor who has been in contact with aliens and thoroughly misunderstood them, and who is later revealed to be – literally – a tool of occult forces. That work is *Out of the Silent Planet* (1938) by CS Lewis. In it and its sequels *Perelandra* (1943) (aka *Voyage To Venus*) and *That Hideous Strength* (1945), marketed under the overall title of **The Cosmic Trilogy**[53], Ransom eventually grows to occupy a position of some sanctity as the logos of Britain, and his name therefore represents his growing to echo the role of Christ – the 'ransom' of the world who sacrifices himself to bear mankind's sins. However, in the first book a more straightforward play on the name is being made, for Ransom is taken to Mars not as a willing explorer, but as a captive by Professor Weston and his associate Devine, as they mistakenly believe that the inhabitants of Mars are barbarians and savages who can best be appeased by offering up to them some (to Weston and Devine) worthless human as a sacrifice. By intervening to free their servant, a boy with learning disabilities, from captivity, Ransom in effect unknowingly offers himself up for this sacrifice in the boy's place.

If we have this in mind, we can see that Thea Ransome is probably going to be sacrificed to something; and her first name, Thea, in Greek means 'goddess' or 'godly' – the female form of 'theos', from which we get 'theology'. Her role then, like Fendelman's later, is plain in her name: she is to be sacrificed to a god – but as the episode unfolds with the impossible skull taking our attention, we do not yet realize how horrible that sacrifice, and how awful that god, will be. Nor that it will be made manifest in Thea's image, as a floating goddess whose torn and tattered robes suggest webs, wings, and a great blank face with tears for eyes.

---

[53] This now seems to have changed to **The Space Trilogy**, for reasons which I don't quite see.

The Impossible Skull: Palaeological Horror

What's going on with palaeoarchaeology and human evolution here? The core of Fendelman's research (as Fendelman himself says later) is the discovery of prehistoric bone fragments (enough to recreate the whole Skull). There is some confusion in the narrative over which came first, the time scanner's results or the dig. In episode 1, 'corrected co-ordinates' are being given by Adam (the archaeologist) to Max Stael (the physicist?), but later Professor Fendelman states that he told Adam where to dig. However, each supports the importance of the restored skull of a seemingly fully human (*Homo sapiens*) specimen recovered from Kenya and dated to 12 million years ago.

This is 'Eustace', as Adam Colby dubs it, and a complete impossibility – at least as a 'free-range' product of unguided evolution.

The origins and evolutionary status of humanity were big topics in popular science in the 1970s and in the televised media, with the first episode of Jacob Bronowski's **The Ascent of Man** (1973) covering prehistory, before moving through the ages of invention in later episodes.

I am convinced that Bronowski's seminal television series is a substantial influence on *Image*. Consider the following:

> 'It is almost certain now that man first evolved in Africa near the equator. Typical of the places where his evolution may have begun is [...] Northern Kenya'[54].

---

[54] Bronowski, Jacob, *The Ascent of Man* (1974), p21. All quotes here come from the book of the series, but Bronowski in his introduction

And, writing of fossil evidence of change: 'The one to concentrate on, of course, is the head.' [55]

Reading Bronowski's account of his measurement of *Australopithecus* teeth, and his modelling of the rates of change to human dentition, in the light of *Image*, is almost to hear the voice of Professor Fendelman:

> 'it transmitted to me a sense of excitement which I remember at this instant. I, at over 40, having spent a lifetime in doing abstract mathematics about the shape of things, suddenly saw my knowledge reach back [...] million[s of] years and shine a searchlight into the history of man.'[56]

Compare this with Fendelman, 10 years before *Image*, working on missile guidance systems when a strange vibration, a 'sonic shadow', sets him on a trail that will let him see into the past.

And again (emphasis mine):

> 'The head is more than a symbolic image of man [...] it is the evolution of **the head and the skull** that has to be traced.'[57]

---

writes: 'In rendering the text used on the screen, I have followed the spoken word closely' (p17). Besides, in an age before the widespread use of private video-recorders, a printed book formed the stored 'reference' of a televised text, and would in 1977 have been the obvious available source for any substantial consultation. (That said, *Lower than the Angels*, episode 1 of **The Ascent of Man** which dealt with prehistory, was repeated on 4 June 1975.)

[55] Bronowski, *The Ascent of Man*, p25.
[56] Bronowski, *The Ascent of Man*, p28.
[57] Bronowski, *The Ascent of Man*, p31.

Writing in 1974, Bronowski sets out the history of human evolution from lemurs (50 million years Before Present (BP)) through anthropoid apes (20 million BP), stating that in *Ramapithecus* (14 million BP, in Kenya):

> 'we are evidently near a branching of the evolutionary tree. [...] There is a blank in the fossil record of five to 10 million years [which hides] the most intriguing part of the story, when the hominid line is firmly separated from the line to the modern apes.'[58]

I believe that the 12 million BP dating for the Skull in *Image* (which has no necessity in the logic of the text, three million or 10 million being as 'possible' as 12) comes from this source – 12 million BP being towards the beginning of a '10 million year blank' or in the middle of a 'five million year blank' – as part of Chris Boucher's concern for verisimilitude. (We will look more closely at the importance of grounding the uncanny in accuracy when we look further at the post-Gothic aspects of *Image*.)

Bronowski's rhapsodies about cave paintings suggest to me the seeds of the time scanner[59]:

> 'They were a peephole into the future [...] in either direction the cave paintings act as a kind of telescope tube of the imagination: they direct the mind from what is seen to what

---

[58] Bronowski, *The Ascent of Man*, p33.

[59] There are of course lots of other time scanners in fiction, including the very early Space-Time Visualiser in **Doctor Who** ('The Executioners (*The Chase* episode 1, 1965)). But I am genuinely struck by how much Bronowski's metaphor matches with Fendelman's technology.

can be inferred or conjectured [...] We also look here through the telescope of the imagination, we are looking back at the experience of the past [...] to move our minds through space and time and to recognize ourselves in the past.'[60]

More Finds by 1977

Writing *Image* in 1977, Chris Boucher could have had Bronowski in mind. He may also have been aware of the discovery in 1974 of 'Lucy' (named after the Beatles track 'Lucy in the Sky with Diamonds'), a substantially intact skeleton of *Australopithecus afarensis* found in Ethiopia. With just over 40% of her bones present, Lucy was a tremendous step forward in understanding human evolution, pushing back our dating for the bipedal form to around 3.2 million BP, a number that would have increased further by 1977. Unlike the pseudo-science writing of Zecharia Sitchin (which is only a possible influence on the fifth planet part of *Image*'s plot, and which we'll look at later), we can be reasonably sure 'Lucy' was in Boucher's mind because 'Leakey', the name he gives to Colby's dog in the story, is that of Mary Leakey, the British palaeoanthropologist involved in the Ethiopian work[61]. In a macabre joke, it is the dog Leakey ('You old bone-hunter, you') who finds the body of the hiker.

---

[60] Bronowski, *The Ascent of Man*, p44.

[61] Mary Leakey's family, the Freres, had been abolitionists who had worked against slavery in the 19th century and left 'Free' or 'Freretowns' named after them in India, South Africa, and Kenya. As the wife of Louis Leakey, she helped to found an entire dynasty of Leakey palaeoanthropologists (any of whom the dog might alternatively be named after).

Let's look at what we think we know **now** about human evolution, before we talk further about the fictional presentation of evolution here. Since 1977, when the bipedal form was known to date back at least to 3.75 million BP thanks to Mary Leakey's (and earlier her husband's) work in the Olduvai Gorge, there have been substantial developments in palaeoarchaeology, but the broad scope of the timescale as set out in Bronowski remains generally intact. Some of the missing five to 10 million years has however been explored: we can be fairly certain that by 12 million years BP, the branching he writes of had not yet occurred.

Not only were there no modern humans 12 million years ago, there were also no chimpanzees. There were the ancestors of today's gibbons and the ancestors of today's great apes, the latter split into two groups: the ancestors of today's orang-utans and another branch consisting of the ancestors of humanity, chimpanzees and gorillas. The 'great ape' group, the 'Hominoidea', and the ancestral gibbons had split between 15 and 20 million BP, and the orang-utans had separated genetically by 14 million BP.

Our direct ancestors, together with those of the chimpanzees, were at that point still within the Gorillini gene-pool, and wouldn't diverge into the separate Hominini (comprising the ancestors of both modern humans and modern chimpanzees) until about eight million years BP. Chimps (Panina) and Hominia would then move away genetically from each other around 7.5 million BP. The 12 million BP dating has therefore become less 'possible' as a major hinge point in human evolution – but in 1977 both the division into Gorillini and Hominini, and the later division into Gorillini, Panina, and Hominia were up for grabs and could easily have occurred at or around 12 million years previously.

Both now and in 1977, an educated audience would have been quick to recognize the general possibility of 12 million years BP representing an important time for human evolution, while seeing the impossibility of Eustace the 'modern man' being present. The cliché of bad/popular prehistoric fiction – of humans co-existing with the Dinosauria hundreds of millions of years ago, of dinosaurs hanging around long enough to still pester a bikini-clad Rachel Welch in *One Million Years BC* (1966) or even (for **Doctor Who** hasn't entirely escaped this) pre-hominid ape-men raiding dinosaur-riding Silurians' crops in a backstory set anywhere between 444 million BP (the start of the Silurian Period) and 33.9 million BP (the end of the Eocene Epoch)[62] – is not used here. *Image*'s historical science is as accurate as popular 1970s sources allowed.

Whatever 'Eustace' is then, we – and the scientifically-literate part of the television audience of the day – would have known and accepted that he couldn't be the skull of a native human *Homo sapiens* of the period. Nor is he presented as such in the story. His impossibility is the first important thing about him – and given the early revelation, in the first scene to include the Doctor and Leela, that this is a story involves a 'time fissure', the audience is invited to suspect that 'Eustace' may turn out to **literally** be the skull of a modern man: of Adam Colby, Max Stael, or Professor Fendelman. In a more 'timey-wimey' era of **Doctor Who**, it is tempting to imagine such a paradox forming part of the resolution of events. Given Chris Boucher's playing with names, it would also have been possibly for the luckless source of Eustace to turn out to be **Adam**

---

[62] *Doctor Who and the Silurians* (1971).

Colby, who would then literally be the first man. (It speaks well, incidentally, for Colby's likeability and lack of pretension as a character, that as the discoverer of the earliest known skull of a true human he hasn't apparently even considered giving it his own first name, and calling it 'Adam'[63].) We'll later see such a time paradox in one of the earliest science fiction stories to make use of the idea of a fifth planet.

We eventually learn how the Skull came to be there, 12 million years ago, and what it has been doing – but we learn it always in the form of speculation, admittedly from the Doctor, who is generally shown in this period (when he's not name dropping, or tricking an adversary) to be truthful about things like scientific theories. According to his best guess: 12 million years ago, as the fifth planet was breaking up (we'll learn this wasn't exactly what happened, but bear with me if I deal with that in its own section) a creature from the mythology of the Time Lords called the Fendahl (which is somehow also known of in legends on this planet) sent part of itself across space from 'the fifth planet' to prehistoric Earth. It was a gestalt creature and the Skull is the remains of a 'Fendahl Core': a part which, when surrounded and upheld by the linked power of 12 other humanoids transformed into Fendahleen, becomes the Fendahl proper – a creature that feeds on life itself, and which can be thought of as a personification of Death.

---

[63] In my **Doctor Who** spinoff novel *Ghost Devices* (1996) I referred to the find as 'Fendleman's Man', only to be criticised for the fact that the find was entirely secret, and lost – but I tend to think that Fendelman would always have had off-site records of his work and theories, and that he would have been the type to insist on scientific immortality if no other could have been had.

I'm just going to say it: that's a brilliant conceit for a monster – and setting aside its realization for a moment, it's a brilliant monster. It's ancient, it's awful, it makes its victims part of itself. Its implications are worse than that.

Consider the two possible explanations of Eustace for humanity. Both of these agree implicitly with what is stated in the story as to how the skull comes to be. Whichever one you take as right leads to appalling consequences for what might be called the 'uniqueness' or the 'individual dignity' of human evolution, and forms a blow at the idea of mankind being formed in the 'image' of God.

This is why I said earlier that if Mrs Mary Whitehouse had understood *Image* she might have found it far more offensive than a few mere strangulations and a toy with a dagger.

We know that modern humans are still not quite right as potential Fendahl Cores – we know this because the Skull has to 'restructure' Thea's brain, projecting into existence as it does so Fendahleen which kill the hiker and Mitchell, and feed it with the life-energy it needs. This suggests that the Skull (which is exactly that of a modern human), might not in fact be exactly that of the original Fendahl Core, but simply the best the projected forces could bring into being from the hominids around it.

In this model some poor hominid was firstly transformed into Eustace, killing it in the process (the moment of its death being recorded as a massive influx of energy by Fendelman's time scanner), and then over millions of years, that template began the work of uplifting enough of the species around it towards that form, so as to drag mankind up to at least that point, after which the reforming gestalt would take over the work of recreating the Fendahl.

If this view is taken as given, we see that something **like** humans, but only in the sense of having large complex brains, evolved on the fifth planet. That evolution ends in a 'dead end' (an idea we'll look at in a moment) with the Fendahl, but its floating, glowing, smiling Core might have looked far less human than the Thea personification at the end of *Image*. In this view, the energy of the Fendahl arriving on Earth did its best to recreate it, torturing at least one early hominid into as close a form as it could. This creature was a thing no doubt grotesque and distorted but able to sustain the gestalt. In this reading we are made in the image of a thing of temporary use, forced and bundled together, and jury-rigged. We are not real, we are a bad copy of an evil thing: a crippled clone of Hitler, a broken Mussolini, the struggling spawn of a demiurge, aping a true God. The actual evolutionary heirs of the Earth are the great apes, who remain on the edge of extinction or in our zoos while we, the distorted image of an alien race, lord it over them.

The alternative – which is a more literal and mechanical reading of the text, and ignores the potential implications of the necessary 'restructuring' of Thea – is that 'Eustace' **is** simply the relic of a Fendahl Core that somehow (by astral travel?) reached Earth. If this is the case then humans – modern *Homo sapiens sapiens* – **did** evolve naturally in the first instance, but **not on Earth**. We evolved on the fifth planet. There we became part of the uppermost species in the food-chain, the Fendahl itself, as it ran its gestalt on a sufficient number of 'human' brains. The evolution that 'turned in on itself' was our own. The thing that lives on Death is us. We are the Fendahl! That is what Mankind became on Planet Five!

This isn't the first time such an idea would have been mooted in a **Doctor Who** context: Terry Nation's short story 'We are the Daleks!' in the *Radio Times* **Doctor Who** 10th anniversary special (1974) suggests that the inhabitants of Skaro came from hominids taken from Earth and evolved by aliens[64]. We look at the monsters and we see the monstrous in ourselves. This is what monsters in **Doctor Who** are for, and the Fendahl takes a throne amongst them with aplomb.

Whichever of these ideas you take as true in the fiction (if either) – whether 'Eustace' was part of the species that grew into a horror, or an ape tortured into the likeness of a monster in order to give that horror rebirth – does not perhaps matter. The energy of the Fendahl, in the psychic circuit – the pentagram within the skull – generates mutations, and places a directing psychic thumb on the random scales of evolution. Not precisely or quickly, but by favouring (via a mechanism that is not stated, but is likely to be destructive rather than constructive, as with Kneale's Martians and their weeding of the genetically unfit or mutated in *Quatermass and the Pit*) mutations that tend towards a complex brain-supporting biped capable of becoming part of the Fendahl, those diverging from it are suppressed or driven away to get on with becoming apes in another part of the forest.

We are what we are because of a skull lying 12 million years ago in Kenya. Not because of a benign God in whose image we were made. Not because of the random chance of an evolution which is

---

[64] *Radio Times*, 24 to 30 November 1973.

at least blameless. We are what we are because an evil that would not die, wished to live again, only to devour – and **that** is true horror.

An Aside: How Does Evolution Work in Doctor Who? Is It Teleological?

Like a lot of popular television science fiction, **Doctor Who** has been at the mercy of authors[65] who are more interested in running quickly with the drama of an idea than necessarily thinking through how it might work, or indeed thinking through whether or not they've even understood the idea. Given that it is a drama not a thesis, this is understandable, if occasionally frustrating.

In *Genesis of The Daleks* (1975) for instance, we see the idea of an ultimate mutational form – what a species will become if it goes on evolving in the present environment for the maximal possible time. In reality there's no such thing, evolution is random and what you get after a million million years is not a predictable result and could (in theory, if the million million years could only be run twice) come out quite differently.

We can, I think, forgive *Genesis* on the grounds that it's a very effective story, Davros is less of a theoretical evolutionary scientist than an ingenious racist genetic engineer/rocket scientist etc, etc, and the environment of Skaro is so blasted with radiation and chemical weapons by this time that a form that could uniquely survive unaided in it might be in a certain specialist sense 'ultimate', if also hideous and blighted.

---

[65] Or blessed with them, depending how you look at it.

Since the 70s the success of evolution as a theory, which has stood up to every piece of fossil evidence, and whose effects can be seen in small-scale evolutionary effects like the appearance of antibiotic-resistant diseases, has meant that attempts to argue against it need to be disguised as science, rather than relying on sticking fingers in ears and going 'Lalalalah I'm not listening, God did it.'

Ironically there is no necessity to disbelieve in evolution to enable belief in God, although it is necessary to disbelieve in evolution to believe in one specific, very weird, fundamentalist subset of Christianity which demands that yes there was an Ark, and a Flood, and literally a single male Adam, and a single female Eve who was made as an afterthought from Adam's rib, and that it all happened in or around 4004 BCE.

The modern form of arguing against evolution is 'Intelligent Design', which holds that it can identify the work of an 'intelligent designer' who may or may not be God by spotting an 'irreducible complexity' in the mechanics, whether biochemical or physical, of an animal or a plant – that is, something that could only work as it is, not in a more primitive form from which it could have evolved.

The horror of such an idea – for which luckily there is no evidence – is that nothing guarantees the benevolence of such a designer, nor even its sentience. The Fendahl is a fictional example of an intelligent designer that bodes us no good, and whose sentience we cannot even judge. In *Image* it never speaks or boasts. It simply absorbs.

In the real world though, so far as we know, **evolution is a non-directed, randomly caused but non-random process**. This gives a lot of people problems – from the ones who want to think of humankind as being 'more evolved' than, say, a slime-mould to the ones who want to deny the whole thing on the grounds that random pairing together of amino acids and stuff shouldn't have made a single cell yet – so let's break it down bit by bit.

Randomly caused means only that a specific mutation in a specific organism doesn't have a causal chain that runs back to a 'purpose'. Animals and plants don't mutate **in order** to do something better, they mutate at random, and mostly the tiny changes are neutral, or worse than the normal operation of the genes affected. Mutated genes are caused by almost any environmental effect, from a hit on the gene by a cosmic ray to toxins in the environment, either natural (shockingly, 'organic' doesn't mean 'safe') or human-made. Mutation is not a cunning plan by an omniscient or nigh-omniscient entity to achieve a specific long-term effect, because its randomness means that it **will** produce an effect but you can't predict what it will be. Mutation is just a thing that happens to anything that includes instructions to replicate copies of itself (where those instructions can vary) – both living things and experimental computer code.

Non-directed means that the effects of evolution are morally equivalent and of equal value. A herbivore is not morally better than a carnivore. A multicellular creature is not more evolved than a unicellular one. A modern herbivore and a modern carnivore are likely to be better adapted to fit the current environmental niche (or, more accurately, are better adapted to fit the niche that existed when they were successfully conceived by parents who had survived until then) than a random ancestor of theirs is likely to be if it could be magically summoned by say, Professor Whitaker's time scoop[66]. Note that this is not to say that a specific ancestor of a modern creature might not **happen** to be better adapted to present conditions that the modern one – that would just mean that its original environment was very similar to modern conditions, although there might have been very different environments in between – but it would be at a definite disadvantage when it came to, say, finding a breeding partner.

Non-random process means that the long-term effect of these random events is not itself random, because living in an environment of different levels of reproductive success applies a sorting filter to the whole population of the animal or plant or microbe concerned. Any mutation that occurs randomly will have an effect on the spread of genetic characteristics in the next generation's population. Which is to say, if a gene **can** be randomly mutated to change how it expresses itself (and we know now that genes can have their 'switches' for the creation of proteins thrown in different ways by the environment, as well through a process called epigenetics) a certain proportion of the population **will** have that change. If that proportion is rendered more able to survive, compete, and breed, even in a small way (just as in other cases mutations that were not useful in these terms depress success), the change will gradually spread through the population, generation after generation, until it becomes the norm or reaches a stable level. (If, for instance, one gene is useful, but two copies of it in one individual are bad, it won't rise above a certain point in the total gene-pool.) Gradually changes (and capacities to change in certain directions) that are beneficial in reproductive terms proliferate, and

---

[66] *Invasion of the Dinosaurs* (1974).

those which are negative or too rigid are placed at a disadvantage and reduce. Over evolutionary time – millions of years – one set of blobs can become trees, snakes, humans, birds, fish or politicians, and one can go on being successful blobs, but all have been subject to evolution. The measure of evolution is not so much that there's a 'top species' called humanity[67] but that the variation in the total biosphere is so vast.

Looking at it this way shows us what 'an evolutionary dead-end' could mean.

Natural evolution is like a tree or a flower opening out: a fractal moving into greater complexity, each bit of it as evolved as the rest, each bit of it a potentially new and stranger and more different life. (Even this is a bit of a misstatement, because there isn't any **necessary** advantage in notional 'higher complexity' in terms of whether a biosphere is successful, but it gives us a tool to look at this issue.) A non-dead end ecology colonises new niches on the fringes of habitability, by adapting at the 'far ends' of its spread of life.

If 'eating life itself' means anything, the Fendahl throws this drive to complexity into reverse. It not only sits atop the food chain, it subverts the stages. It does not just kill the cow and eat the steak; instead it passes through the field, and the cow, and the grass and insects, and the bacteria in the insects' guts, and the worms under the earth, and the spores and the seeds in their seasons all die, and all that energy – all that potential – becomes Fendahl, until only Fendahl is left; and then the Fendahl eat each other, until only one

---

[67] Or by mass, the bacterium – or by numbers of individual multicellular units, the ant or termite.

remains. Does it then launch itself psychically into space to attack a new world? Whether it does so as a biological imperative, or whether that was only its last expedient in the face of the action taken against it by the Time Lords, we can't know.

The SF writer Brian Stableford has published a far-future romance in which he postulates a form of ecology- and consciousness-destroying evolution which he calls 'third-phase life'[68]. This is a type of unthinking unicellular life that makes what it needs as multicellular nodules, and then destroys them and any **other** multicellular life it comes into contact with. Once it evolves on a world, that world is forever doomed as a possible site for the development of consciousness:

> 'In the new biocosm there were no individuals, but only life. There was no competition, save for that between the system and the vicissitudes of its environment. There was no behavioural strategy, save for that of the system as a whole, which was simply to survive and grow, not to reproduce. There was no conceivable need for the evolution of intelligence. And thus it was third-phase life assumed command of the planet called Earth.'[69]

Such life might be called Fendahloid. Both Stableford's third-phase life and the Fendahl hark back to the creatures in *The Quatermass Xperiment* and *Quatermass 2* (and perhaps their American teen cousin *The Blob* (1958)): once they are established on a world, all else is absorbed into, and becomes, them.

---

[68] Brian Stableford, *The Walking Shadow: A Promethean Scientific Romance*, pp130-142.
[69] Stableford, *The Walking Shadow*, p183.

So if evolution is random, what does it mean to say that the Skull is 'becoming a mutation generator' – wouldn't that just make things turn into other things quicker, rather than tending to become Fendahls?

In the real world, yes: if the Skull just put out gamma-rays say, it would cause a lot of mutations and kill a lot of animals, and stand just as much chance of producing a Fendahl as an aardvark, and mostly it would just cause cancers; but this fictional Skull contains a genetic map (either precisely, or in 'get to something we can work with' terms).

If it has some sort of feedback mechanism, it doesn't necessarily have to cause every mutation that created the Fendahl on the fifth planet in the first place. It can cut corners. A recent discovery that might suggest a means is the existence of 'clocks' in living cells which set a rate for mutational buildup – 'a discovery made after the study of more than 10,000 individual cancers[70]'. By increasing cell division in mutational strains tending towards its mapping image, and decreasing it in those tending away, the Fendahl Core could be thought of as increasing the rate at which the Fendahl-prone Apes (humanity) will come into being, while 'freezing' adaptive change in competing genomes. With a science-fictional assumption that an energy can be stored and expended so as to direct evolution, the timescales of *Image* are those of the popularised science of its day, and the ideas are valid extrapolations.

---

[70] Thomson, Helen, 'Death-Clock in Cells Counts Down to Cancer', *New Scientist*, 14 November 2015, p11.

Another Aside: What's the Title All About Again?

The questions the viewer asks him- or herself as they begin to watch the story are, 'What **is** a Fendahl?' and 'What is important about its "image"?' The Fendahl is not a recurring monster, and this story is its one and only television appearance (we will look briefly at the spin-off media which refer to it in Appendix 1, 'Afterimage of the Fendahl'). Its nature will be made clear in the story, but why it's called a 'Fendahl' is less clear.

Some authors must hate being asked how they come up with names for new monsters, or planets or things never seen upon the earth, or even people. Terry Nation invented a story about seeing an encyclopaedia volume that ran from 'DAL' to 'LEK', rather than admit he'd just made the name up[71]. Nigel Kneale, whose influence on *Image* is considerable (if not directly, then via the 'post-Gothic' strand of Hammer Horror), was on the other hand happy to admit looking in a telephone directory for odd names when he was deciding what to name his hero – assuming that story is true.

It is tempting to think that Boucher followed Kneale's example, and that 'Fendahl' is a back-creation from the unusual but real name 'Fendelman' or 'Fendleman'[72]. 'Fendahl' is itself a surname however, albeit an even rarer one[73].

---

[71] Documented in Turner, Alwyn W, *Terry Nation: The Man Who Invented the Daleks* (2011) (Kindle edition), location 184.

[72] In the US the name 'Fendelman' is rare: 73 results across the 1910-1940 census (available at www.findmypast.com). Some of these are multiple counts of the same family member. The name is centred around Missouri and Philadelphia. The 'Fendleman' form used in the novelisation is even rarer, with 10 results. The forenames of many of the 'Fendleman' variant suggest Jewish

Alan Barnes suggests a possible root in 'fend' or 'fende' – archaic Middle English forms of the word 'fiend' as listed in the *Oxford English Dictionary*[74]. Another possibility is the German 'Feondliche', meaning 'hostile' or 'fiend-like'. Google translate – try it – says that 'Fendahl' is German[75], but 'Fendhal' is Javanese, but won't translate either one. (An alternative source for 'Fendahleen', in the sense of a subordinate or lower form of the main creature, might be the Egyptian term 'fellaheen', the plural of 'fellah', a native labourer or peasant.)

I believe, however, that I have identified the 'real' Fendelman and the pun that may have partly suggested the story, in an American computer scientist and businessman of the 1970s: Doctor Gene

---

ancestry (the first record I found is Lewin Fendleman, born c1892 Russia, 1940 residence Missouri). It is possible that Fendelman's rather strange accent is Russian moderated by an American upbringing. There seem to be no Fendelmans or Fendlemans in the UK according to www.ancestry.co.uk, although a family of five left the UK for New York in 1910.

[73] There is a 'Miss A Fendahl' in the US census for 1910, born about 1840 in Wisconsin. The last UK Fendahl, Miss MMH Fendahl, born about 1900, left the UK in 1927 for New Zealand. (Sadly, she there takes her husband's name and the descent of the Fendahl vanishes from easy scrutiny.) There was also a small cluster of Fendahls in Illinois. In some cases 'Fendahl' is given as a variant of 'Fenski'. (Worryingly, while looking this up online I find there is a Fendahl Technology Limited: Fendelman's heirs and wider family may have continued his electronic work.)

[74] Barnes, 'The Fact of Fiction'.

[75] The German surname 'Dahl', which also forms a suffix as a component of names, means 'valley' and is from the same root as 'dale' in English. The 'Thal' in 'Neanderthal' also comes from this root.

Amdahl. 'He was the founder of the Amdahl Corporation which became a major rival to IBM in the mainframe market during the 1970s and 80s.'[76] Amdahl's first customer was NASA's Goddard Spaceflight Centre[77]. Remembering Boucher's playing with names in *Robot of Death,* I find it quite conceivable that a multimillionaire electronics genius, associated with rocketry – whose forename 'Gene' suggests evolutionary biology, and whose last name 'Amdahl' could have formed part of the genesis of 'Fendahl' – may have inspired Professor Fendelman.

What Is the 'Image' in *Image of the Fendahl*?

Some **Doctor Who** story titles are simply descriptive. (*The Planet of the Daleks* is about a Planet of Daleks. *The Horror of Fang Rock is* about a Horror that occurs on Fang Rock.)

Others are metaphors that are explained in literal terms within the dialogue of the show. ('The Claws of Axos are buried deep in the carcass of the earth, soon they will begin to feed.')

Is the 'Image' in *Image of the Fendahl* the ghostly image of Thea, superimposed upon the Skull? Or the transparent Fendahleen appearing as miniature phantom worms atop her body? Or the image it has implanted of itself, in the core of all our cells? It is of course, all three. It is the God in whose image we have been made. The image of the Fendahl is what we see in a mirror.

This view is also taken by Graham Sleight, who writes: 'Like so many other monsters in the series the effect of the Fendahl is to

---

[76] O'Regan, Gerald, *Giants of Computing: A Compendium of Select, Pivotal Pioneers*, p13.
[77] O'Regan, *Giants of Computing*, p15.

make humans monstrous. The lucky ones like Stael realise what they've done.'[78]

---

[78] Graham Sleight, *The Doctor's Monsters: Meanings of the Monstrous in Doctor Who* (2012), p176.

CHAPTER 4: THE POST-GOTHIC AND THE COSMOS

'The Doctor buys time with an ancient charm - but needs to harness the most dangerous modern equipment if he is to defeat the Fendahl and save mankind.'[79]

[*Radio Times*]

The single greatest initiator of what I'm calling post-Gothic horror in US literature is HP Lovecraft. In his letters he writes about his writing, and how he considers a story should function:

> 'To achieve the essence of real externality, whether of time or space or dimension, one must forget that such things as organic life, good and evil, love and hate, and all such local attributes of a negligible and temporary race called mankind, have any existence at all. Only the human scenes and characters must have human qualities. **These** must be handled with unsparing **realism**, (not catch-penny **romanticism**) but when we cross the line to the boundless and hideous unknown-the shadow-haunted **Outside** – we must remember to leave our humanity and terrestrialism at the threshold.'[80]

Although the term 'Lovecraftian' has come to be used for this mode of horror, I consider it, in fact, the same as the post-Gothic – and Lovecraft owed a substantial debt to Edgar Allen Poe, to Arthur Machen, and Ambrose Blackwood (as well as, on the fantasy side,

---

[79] *Radio Times*, 12 to 18 November 1977.
[80] HP Lovecraft, *Selected Letters* vol 2, p150.

Lord Dunsany). He side-stepped a direct debt to the Gothic, reading *Otranto* and others of the form for the first time in 1926, after 'Dagon' had already been written – but he absorbed it at one remove through the authors he already loved[81].

However, in his work, elements from Machen, Blackwood, Poe, and Dunsany fuse into something sufficiently characteristic to deserve a new description. The essence of this horror is the vastness of its scope, and its refusal to rely on the traditional monsters of the Gothic – the vampire, the werewolf, the mummy[82]. Instead it treads a path of careful rationalism and normality in the foreground, while preparing as its evil surprise to kick away every comforting notion about humanity's value, or capacity to survive. Its basis is not that aliens may kill or destroy us in a physical sense – although they may – but that the discovery of their existence and their nature so alters our perception of what the world is and how it functions, that it will end our bright hopes of understanding the universe, or of finding any resting-place in it. This is most obviously

---

[81] Lovecraft's account of his reading can be found in *Letters to James F Morton*, ed David E Schultz and ST Joshi. (For instance he did not read Robert W Chambers' *The King in Yellow* until long after the invention of his own maddening occult book, *The Necronomicon*.)

[82] The Ghoul does make it into Lovecraft, but his meeping, Dog-faced Ghouls – who nevertheless can be reasoned with, and can crack a sardonic joke (laughing at a guidebook's statement that 'Holmes, Lowell, and Longfellow Lie Buried in Mount Auburn' because they know they've eaten them), are – as they appear in Pickman's paintings and Carter's dreams at least – a creation in their own right (Lovecraft, HP, 'Pickman's Model' and 'The Dream-Quest of Unknown Kadath', in *The Necronomicon*) .

summed up by the opening lines of 'The Call of Cthulhu' (emphasis mine):

> 'The most merciful thing in the world, I think, is the inability of the human mind to correlate all its contents. We live on a placid island of ignorance in the midst of black seas of infinity, and it was not meant that we should voyage far. The sciences, each straining in its own direction, have hitherto harmed us little; but **some day the piecing together of dissociated knowledge will open up such terrifying vistas of reality, and of our frightful position therein, that we shall either go mad from the revelation or flee from the deadly light into the peace and safety of a new dark age.**'[83]

The whole thrust and intent of Lovecraft's horror is to make this sentiment concrete and believable. In doing so, he advised, a horror writer should approach the unbelievable by grounding it as much as possible, by approaching it in the same way as a hoaxer attempting to carry off a con, and he was pleased (though at times irritated) by his success in making his fictional props seem realistic, as when he was required to answer again an awestruck letter from a fan pleading for the actual release of a transcription of the *Necronomicon*.

Alan Moore concurs with this view:

> 'With Lovecraft I think that it's a much more present horror of the future. He's talking about that time when

---

[83] Lovecraft, HP, *The Necronomicon: The Best Weird Fiction of H.P. Lovecraft*, p201.

man will be able to organize all of his knowledge. And [...] whether we will flee from it [...] Which is very prescient given, say, current fundamentalism, which is a direct – a response to too much knowledge, too much information. Let's take it all back to something that we're sure of: God created the world in six days. Yeah, in that way Lovecraft [...] is still a very contemporary writer.'[84]

Thomas Ligotti – a modern writer of disturbing philosophical horror – has separately identified the 'literal' or 'grounded' (my post-Gothic) approach as one of three 'primary techniques that authors have employed to produce tales of terror,' the others being 'the traditional Gothic technique, and the experimental technique'[85].

Of the literal technique, Ligotti writes:

'in order to achieve this effect, the supernatural realist must really know the normal world and deeply take for granted its reality [...] only then can the unreal, the abnormal, the supernatural be smuggled in as a plain brown package marked Hope, Love or Fortune Cookies, and postmarked: the Edge of the Unknown.'[86]

The paradox of the successful style of horror we now call Lovecraftian, is that the effects of the supposed supernatural upon the reader – the effect which CS Lewis describes as 'numinous' – is produced by things which are not in themselves numinous. The distinction Lewis suggests is that if you really believed there was a

---

[84] Doctorow, 'Alan Moore on Lovecraft and the 20th Century'.

[85] Thomas Ligotti, 'Notes On The Writing Of Horror' in *Songs of a Dead Dreamer* (2012) (Kindle edition), location 1630.

[86] Ligotti, 'Notes On The Writing Of Horror', location 1640.

tiger in the next room you would be afraid, but not in awe or shaken, whereas if you really believed there was a ghost or a mighty spirit in the next room you would be in awe, and shaken, even if you weren't afraid[87]. Lovecraft's sleight of hand – his ability to have his cake and eat it – is to postuate something in the next room that is non-supernatural (because it's alien) but is **so** alien, so old, so powerful, so strange, so 'other', that it produces the response appropriate to the uncanny. (A driving component to this is Lovecraft's own pathological racism – but luckily there is no trace of that in *Image* and we need not address this topic here.)

The Fendahl can be thought of as a Lovecraftian creation, not just because it's icky and has (sort of) tentacles at its open maw, but because its existence changes our view of how we came to be, how our solar system is arranged, and what place we fit in the great food-chain of the universe – where, as another toiler in the Lovecraftian vineyard once wrote: 'We are the plankton of the seas of space and time.'[88]

Astronomy in *Image*

One of Lovecraft's earliest passions was astronomy, and he was quick to bring the cosmic as an element into his fiction. ST Joshi has suggested that the continual increase in the best scientific

---

[87] Lewis, CS, *The Problem of Pain* included in *The Complete CS Lewis Signature Classics* (2012) (Kindle edition), location 4576.
[88] Lumley, Brian, 'Born of the Winds', included in *The Taint and Other Novellas* (2008), p92.

estimates of the size of the cosmos over Lovecraft's lifetime contributed to his sense of isolation and unease[89].

What the does the science of *Image* tells us about our Solar System? How accurate (or believable – for the two things are not necessarily the same) is it? And how does the world it depicts disturb **our** comfortable beliefs? We've already looked at the palaeoarchaeology of *Image* and seen that it is – up to the point of its single impossibility (the Skull) – accurate, depicting what the audience would have expected as fact, to the point needed to ground its attack on humanity's self-image. Let's now have a look at the astronomy of *Image* and see if that does the same.

Popular Astronomy, Or Why Did We Think There Should Have Been a Fifth Planet?

In *Image* the titular menace comes from the fifth planet of the Solar System, a mythical world that once existed between Earth and Mars. How likely is this idea, and where did it originate? Well surprisingly, perhaps, it comes from absolutely genuine cutting-edge science, albeit that of the 18th century.

Even before its falsity was proven, astronomical observations had shown that the simple geocentric model of the Solar System, which had bodies going around the Earth rather than the Sun, didn't work, or if it did it worked in a counter-intuitive way.

Sometimes the planets would appear to go backwards. (We now know this is because the planets, including the Earth, orbit the Sun

---

[89] 'Time, Space and Natural Law: Science and Pseudo-Science in Lovecraft' in Joshi, ST, *Lovecraft and a World in Transition: Collected Essays* (2014) (Kindle edition), locations 3578-4093.

at different speeds and a planet viewed from Earth will appear to slow and then move backwards in its orbit as the Earth in its orbit moves faster, and 'ahead' of the other.) To explain this with a stationary Earth, a complicated system of epicycles was needed to predict the planets' movements[90]. These worked as if planets were themselves orbiting around 'points' which then orbited the Earth – or (in Tycho Brache's intermediate schema between geocentric and heliocentric[91]) as if they orbited an Earth which itself orbited the Sun. These schemata were immensely fiddly and mathematically difficult, but could be made to work.

The size of the epicycle needed can be shown to bear a relationship to the actual orbital size in the simpler (and, as it happens, true) heliocentric model. Because of this, although the true distances of the planets were not worked out fully, the **relative** distances of the known planets from the Sun were clear from around the 16th Century. This is perhaps not surprising, because the epicycle radius is a way of modelling, from the point of view of the Earth's orbit, the parallax of the different planets. As soon as you've got even the relative distances of the planets worked out, something very odd shows up.

For the first four planets, Mercury, Venus, Earth and Mars, there appears to be a simple pattern in their distances from the Sun, which breaks down for Jupiter and Saturn.

---

[90] Berry, Arthur, *A Short History of Astronomy* (2012) (Kindle edition), p121.
[91] Thoren, Victor E, *The Lord of Uraniborg: A Biography of Tycho Brahe* (1991), pp236-264.

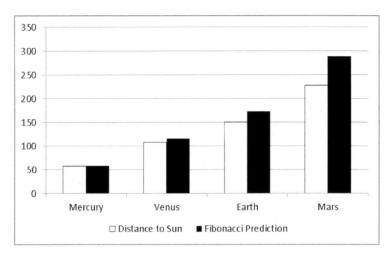

Figure 1: *Average distance from Sun of planets in millions of kilometres, versus prediction based on the Fibonacci sequence, from Mercury baseline.*

The distances of the worlds from the Sun appear to follow a mathematical rule of thumb. The sequence is like the Fibonacci number sequence: (0), 1, 1, 2, 3, 5, 8 – where each number is the sum of the preceding two. This number sequence was discovered (or at least popularised in Europe in 1202 CE, for the discoverer may have been an Arab mathematician) by Leonardo Bonnacci, also known as Fibonacci, or Leonardo of Pisa[92]. Formulated as a description of the breeding pattern of (ideal, immortal, mathematical) rabbits, it predates the measurement of the distances to the planets, but it offers a rule of thumb against which, once known, the first four of them stack up remarkably well. The

---

[92] Solomon, Dr Robert, *The Little Book of Mathematical Principles* (2008), pp54-55.

rounded average distances from the Sun as we now know them are:

- **Mercury** 57 million km (35 million miles)
- **Venus** 108 million km (67 million miles)
- **Earth** 150 million km (93 million miles)
- **Mars** 228 million km (142 million miles)
- **Jupiter** 779 million km (484 million miles)
- **Saturn** 1.43 billion km (889 million miles)[93].

The planets move in ellipses and are not all at their average distance from the Sun at the same time, but the Fibonacci number sequence is found in many parts of nature[94], and for the first four worlds the fit is close enough to suggest the discovery of a natural law of planetary formation. However, extending it to Jupiter and Saturn causes it to break down.

---

[93] Moore, Patrick, and Garry Hunt, *The Atlas of the Solar System* (1990), pp78, 100, 132, 212, 248, 314; confirmed at 'Distances Between the Planets' (2016).

[94] Including the mathematical 'Golden Ratio' and the number of petals in many plants (Solomon, *The Little Book of Mathematical Principles*, pp54-55).

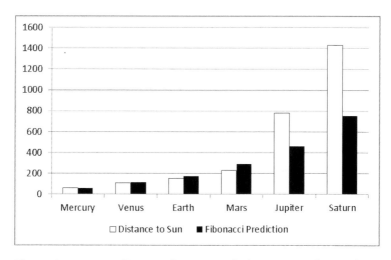

Figure 2: *Average distance from Sun of planets in millions of km, versus prediction based on Fibonacci sequence, from Mercury baseline, showing apparent breakdown of progression for Jupiter and Saturn*[95].

1766: A new approach

In 1766 Johann Daniel Titus (and Johann Elert Bode, who publicised it in a footnote in his work *An Instructive Guide to Knowledge of the Starry Heavens (Anleitung zur Kenntniss des gestirnten Himmels)*[96] (1768)) proposed an alternative mathematical way of predicting

---

[95] While wrong, this was still far better than estimates based on the old celestial sphere model, which put Saturn at 19,900 Earth radii away, or 76 million miles (122 million kilometres) from Earth, which is to say only just past Mars (Neugebauer, O, *A History of Ancient Mathematical Astronomy* vol 1 (1976), pp 917–926).

[96] It's a minor point of resonance that Lovecraft's story 'The Haunter of The Dark' includes 'The Starry Wisdom Church' (*The Necronomicon* p607).

planetary orbits. This follow an earlier work by Charles Bonnet which Titus translated – however, just as with Fibonacci, it was Titus and Bode who were given the credit of having their names attached to the idea thereafter, and it became known as 'the Titus-Bode Hypothesis' (or sometimes, as Bode was pushier, 'Bode's Law').

Their method was based on recent calculations of Saturn's orbit, and involved working backwards, dividing the distance from Saturn to the Sun into 100 'units' – after which, they observed, the Sun to Mercury accounted for 4 units, Venus 4 + 3 (= 7), the Earth 4 + 6 (= 10), Mars 4 + 12 (= 16), a hypothetical fifth planet 4 + 24 (28), Jupiter 4 + 48 (= 52) and Saturn 4 + 96 (= 100), doubling the distance from the Mercury baseline each time. They predicted **both** a planet beyond Saturn at 4 + 192 (= 196) and a fifth planet at 4 + 24 (= 28), that is 28 / 100 of the distance to Saturn, or 248 million miles (400 million km). (I have added a prediction which they did not make of a further planet, because we'll have need of that before too long when we're testing their methodology.)

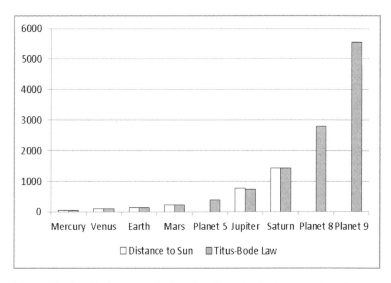

Figure 3: *Predictions made by the Titus-Bode law against known observations of Solar System, 1766.*

This method gave very close matches for the orbital distances of all the known planets in 1766, and very strong testable predictions.

However, the more cautious reader will realize that this match is basically Bode and Titus's own construct. The choice to work back from Saturn, the choice of what percentage to apply and the choice of what number to start with (why is Mercury 4?) and how much to increase each step by (if 2 X 3 hadn't worked, why couldn't it have been 1.8 X 3?) are essentially assignable at will, until a good match with observations appears.

Construct or not, in 1781 the discovery of a planet beyond Saturn (Planet 8 in the above schema) seemed to vindicate Bode and Titus and prove that there was an underlying mathematical regularity to the Solar System. That planet was Uranus.

The pinpointing of this new planet (which we accredit to William Herschel although it may well have been observed many times before but misidentified as a star, and a counter-claim for primacy by the French astronomer Pierre Lemonnier predates Herschel by 10 years) **seemed** to prove Titus-Bode's Law. 196 / 100 of Saturn's distance was 1,742 million miles (2,803 million km), and Uranus's orbit was on average 1,710 million miles (2,752 million km). This was a 98% accurate prediction.

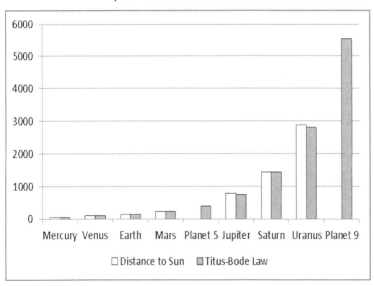

Figure 4: *Apparent vindication of Titus-Bodes Law with discovery of Uranus where predicted! (1781).*

From the seven known planets then, the temptation to imagine that the distances of the planets as astronomers knew them were so because of underlying mathematical rules was a substantial one. (It may even still be true – we do not yet have any other solar systems we can consider in parallel. While modern techniques can, by looking for 'wobbles' in starlight caused by planets passing in front of their stars, detect large worlds, and we now know of hundreds of big extrasolar planets, we cannot as yet detect small rocky planets of earth size or less. Because of this, all the known extrasolar planets thus far discovered are gas giants or 'super-earths', and we do not yet have a complete map of even one other star system. Indeed we do not yet have a completely definitive map of our own[97].

But to return to the 18th century...

If There Was an Eighth Planet in the Right Place, What of The Fifth?

The apparent rule means that we should expect to have seen from prehistoric times – orbiting at a distance of Earth plus Mars from the Sun, or thereabouts – a fifth planet. That would be 92 + 142, or around 234 million miles (377 million km) (Fibonacci), or (4 + 24) /100 the orbit of Saturn, 249 million miles (400 million km) (Titus-Bode).

After the discovery of Uranus, Titus, Bode and others petitioned astronomers to seek (and themselves sought) for evidence of a fifth planet between Mars and Jupiter, in the position predicted. Perhaps it existed but had a very low albedo (reflectivity) and was simply hard to observe?

---

[97] Just after I wrote this, a suggestion was publicised to the effect that there might be a 'super-earth' hitherto undetected in Trans-Neptunian space. Koberlein, Brian, 'Astronomers Find New Object, Possible Super-Earth in Our Solar System' (2015).

Could There Be a Dark Missing World Within the Sun's Family of Planets?

In January 1801, Ceres was discovered by Giuseppe Piazzi. It's large enough to now be classed as a 'dwarf planet' (although this is mainly a category invented by nostalgic astronomers wanting to retain the term 'planet' for a class of body that would continue to include Pluto, following its 'demotion' in 2006)[98]. Its average orbit of 257 million miles (443 million km) seemed close enough to be final proof of the Titus-Bode law, and it was initially hailed, without any qualification, as a planet!

At the beginning of the 19th Century, the 'official' list of planets in the Solar System went: Mercury, Venus, Earth, Mars, Ceres, Jupiter, Saturn, and Uranus, and the Titus-Bode law was considered a fact of nature.

---

[98] 'The Dwarf Planet Ceres'.

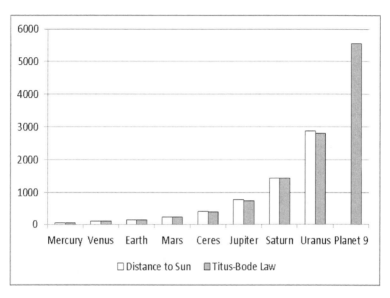

Figure 5: *The Solar System from 1801 CE to the first three months of 1802 CE.*

That lasted all of a year and three months (because this was an exciting time for astronomy). The discoveries of Pallas (1802), Juno (1804) and Vesta (1807) in pretty much the same orbit as Ceres made it clear that that something very odd was going on. Planets just **weren't** found that close together, and the tool being used to find them – Titus-Bode's law itself – said that they **couldn't** be. As early as 1802, Herschel suggested that Ceres and Pallas were **not** planets and needed a different name. He coined the word 'asteroid' – from the Greek for 'image of a star', or 'star-like'. It would be 40 years, though, before his term was commonly adopted, due to a minor interruption to peaceful astronomy known as the Napoleonic Wars. This used up resources, and disrupted research, including – tragically for science – the burning in 1813 of the observatory of Lilenthal near Bremen, which had been most involved in the discovery of Pallas and Juno. It was not until 1845 that astronomers could begin looking for more asteroids, and the fifth, Astraea, was discovered.

We now know that Ceres comprises about one-third of the mass of all bodies orbiting between Mars and Jupiter, and that there are at least 200,000 bodies[99] in what is now called 'the asteroid belt', massing in total perhaps 4% to 5% of the mass of Earth's Moon.

Why, Then, Were There Planets Everywhere the Rule Predicted, Except in One Place Where There Were Four Or More Smaller Bodies?

Two theories rapidly came to dominate the discussion. In one model (which we currently accept, although with some possible variations), when the planets formed, the gravity of the largest planet, Jupiter, was sufficiently strong to perturb the masses orbiting between Mars and Jupiter either outward past Jupiter, and hence out of the Solar System, or having orbited Jupiter, by slingshot back into the inner solar system, with the result that while small bodies – the asteroids – did form, no large planet came into being in the gap. This theory accounts for the very small amount of mass remaining in the orbit, it having (in respective order of predominance) been captured by Jupiter, been flung from the Solar System, or fallen into the Sun, with only a proportion remaining.

The second, rather more dramatically fanciful theory (that of Wilhelm Olbers[100], the astronomer who discovered Pallas), was

---

[99] Some sources say 500,000 (Major, Jason, 'How Many Asteroids are Out There?').

[100] 'Wilhelm Olbers', *Encyclopaedia Britannica*.

that a properly-sized planet, perhaps the size of Mars or larger – a rocky world, like the inner planets rather than the outer gas giants – had once existed within the Titus-Bode orbit predicted for the fifth planet, but that at some point a catastrophe had occurred to shatter it into the asteroids seen today.

The weakness of such a theory, apart from the absence of any known reason for the destruction, was that the timescale involved would have to allow for the formation of the planet and a period of existence long enough to encompass the likelihood of its destruction, then still leave long enough again for the removal from the orbit of all but four to five 'Moon-hundredths' of its mass, without any of the other planets being destroyed in the interim. Still, the fifth planet was a definite theory, of a real scientist. That theory, and Titus-Bode's law, lasted another 60 years – until Neptune was found in the wrong place!

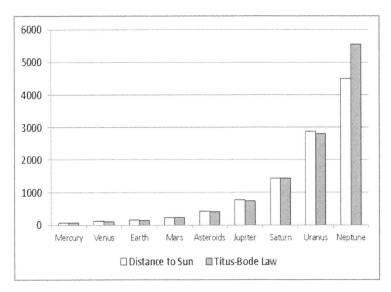

Figure 6: *The discovery of Neptune (1846) puts a spoke in this wheel.*

After Neptune it seemed that Titus-Bode, like Fibonacci before it, did not actually map the Solar System. While the gap between prediction and average orbit for Neptune doesn't look too large in this scale, it's a bigger gap than the distance between the Sun and Jupiter.

Bonus Astronomy Extra! Vulcan

A further astronomical theory of tangential importance to **Doctor Who** was suggested by Le Verrier in 1860, when his analysis of the orbit of Mercury showed peculiarities which he believed could be explained by a further planet between Mercury and the Sun. He named this world 'Vulcan' – backing up his theoretical justification with a claimed sighting of the planet in transit of the Sun by the amateur astronomer Edmond Modeste Lescarbault on 26 March 1859.

A planet named Vulcan appears in *The Power of The Daleks* (1966), and, while its position is never established, its colonisation by 2020 – the usual dating attributed to the serial – is suggestive of it being a world in our Solar System. The orbit of 21 million miles (34 milllion km) attributed to it by Le Verrier would fit with a negative extension of the Titus-Bode method: (4 - 1.5) / 100 of Saturn's orbit = 22.2 million miles.

Planet Five in Fiction before October 1977

Although it now seems likely that there never was a Planet Five, the dramatic image of an exploding ('disrupted') world appealed to writers, and over time the missing world acquired a number of possible names, and descriptions. I'll touch briefly here on the main ones written before *Image,* that I've been able to inspect.

In *Seola* (1878) by Anne Eliza Smith – a novel set before the biblical flood, told as by a 4,000-year-old manuscript:

> 'Obora, [Angelic] Prince of the Upper Sphere [has]...In his circle a great planet between the Red World and the Green, uninhabited, cracked and fissured deep-seamed and rent by volcanic fire.' [101]

> 'Astronomers inform us that a great planet once existed between Mars and Jupiter which was shattered, and that

---

[101] Smith, Anne Eliza, *Seola* (1878) (Kindle edition), location 1345.

the fragments called asteroids, are now to be seen in that portion of the solar system.'[102]

This 'fifth planet' is between Mars ('Red') and Jupiter ('Green'). It's destruction in a war between Lucifer's rebellious angels (here 'Devas') and the powers of the Eternal leads to the Great Flood.

(The colour green for Jupiter strikes a modern reader as odd, but may conceivably follow Chaucer's 'Canon Yeoman's Tale', where Jupiter's alchemic metal is noted as 'tin', which according to Richard Anthony Proctor's Myths and Marvels of Astronomy equates to 'mixed red and green'[103]. An English astronomer, Proctor produced some of the earliest maps of Mars in 1867, and was a contemporary of Anne Eliza Smith.)

Implicitly there are seven worlds at this time, Earth not being counted as among the planets:

'Quenched is one lamp of the Burning Seven, vacant the place of the Wan Planet and lost forever the bright constellation that madly plunged to outer darkness.' [104]

...which suggests that Smith considered Neptune, if she knew of it, as biblically uncanonical.

Phaeton the son of Helios, who drove his father's burning horses too hard and had to be slain by Zeus to prevent the crashing of the

---

[102] Smith, *Seola*, location 2602 (Author's own footnote).
[103] Proctor, Richard A, *Myths and Marvels of Astronomy* (Kindle edition), location 425.
[104] Smith, *Seola*, Kindle location 1831.

chariot of the Sun, was proposed as a name for Planet Five by the Russian astronomer Sergei Orloff[105] .

The science fiction writer Ross Rocklynne (a pen name of Ross Louis Rocklin) makes an ingenious use of the exploded-world theory in his story 'Time Wants a Skeleton' (*Astounding Science Fiction*, 1941). In the story the protagonists find a skeleton millions of years old in a cave on asteroid 1007, only to accidentally travel back in time (a result of their newly experimental gravity drive) to when the planet was still in existence, to face the horrifying prospect of one of them needing to becoming the skeleton to complete the paradox of 'a human skeleton [that] existed before the human race existed.'[106] They are returned to their own time by the gravity disruption when the planet breaks up, and the story ends bathetically, but before its joke ending it achieves a creepy power with its apparent early use of a 'predestination paradox'.

In *Space Cadet* (1948) by Robert Heinlein, the 'first proof that the asteroids used to be a planet'[107] is the definite presence of sedimentary rock in some specimens. There the disaster is considered to have occurred 'nearly half a billion years ago, [with] most of the ruined planet [having] escaped from the System entirely.'[108] The discoveries made in the novel by the crew of the lost ship *Pathfinder* on 1987-CD, 'a smallish asteroid about a mile in diameter', lead to 'the unmistakable conclusion that the disrupted

---

[105] 'One of our Planets Is Missing', *The Galaxy Express*.
[106] Rocklynne, Ross, 'Time Wants A Skeleton' (1941) in Asimov, Isaac, Charles G Waugh and Martin H Greenberg, *The Mammoth Book of Golden Age SF* (2007) (Kindle edition), locations 226-1367.
[107] Heinlein, Robert, *Space Cadet*, p144.
[108] Heinlein, *Space Cadet*, p150.

planet was inhabited,' and that the planet, which humans have named Lucifer, 'was disrupted by artificial nuclear explosion. In other words, they did it themselves.'

Captain WE Johns (the pen-name of William Earl Johns, better known now for the **Biggles** books) gave Planet Five the hostage-to-catastrophe name of 'Kraka'. (Given such worlds in **Doctor Who** as Aridius – a waterworld that becomes a desert – this sort of naming does seem to attract bad luck.) In the second book in his **Kings of Space** series, *Return to Mars* (1955), a Martian refugee from a civilisation now based around Ceres ('Lentos' in his language) tells Johns' heroes – space travellers from Earth – about the prehistoric destruction of Kraka, whose side-effects devastated Mars[109].

Brian Lumley, in his collection of stories *The Caller of The Black* (1971), names it 'Thyop' and blames its destruction on Azathoth, the mindless God responsible for the cosmos in Lovecraft's cycle of myth[110].

Isaac Asimov in his mystery short story 'The Ultimate Crime' (1976) which turns on a literary puzzle, leaves Planet Five unnamed but suggested that it was the asteroid in Professor Moriarty's thesis *The Dynamics of An Asteroid*[111], and that the evil Professor's intent in his rarefied paper was to discover how that lost world was

---

[109] I read the book as a child, but my memories are confirmed at 'Return to Mars'.

[110] Lumley, Brian, *The Caller of The Black* (1971), p167.

[111] Mentioned in Conan Doyle, Arthur, *The Valley of Fear* (1914).

shattered by some prehistoric super-Moriarty, in order to hold Sherlock Holmes's Earth to ransom[112].

The SF writer James P Hogan called it 'Minerva' in his **Giants** series (beginning with *Inherit the Stars* (May 1977)). In those books the moon of Minerva, blasted out of its orbit in the destruction of its primary, eventually becomes our Moon, and the preserved alien artefacts, and a space-suited body, found there rework our whole understanding of the prehistory of the solar system, including the genetic origins of mankind. The time-scale of television and novel production probably precludes this being an influence on *Image* (broadcast October to November 1977), but it does have some similarities.

In all these stories, the destruction of Planet Five is a consequence of war and folly, either the inhabitants' own or visited on them by a wider 'War in Heaven'. Bones and relics bring a reassessment of the history, or fate, of mankind, and in Rocklynne's story an existential and maddening fear.

The Fifth Planet in Ufology and Pseudoscience

The fifth planet is to ufology what Atlantis, the Hollow Earth, Agartha, and Dimension X are – **another** possible source for UFOs, 'Alien Big Cats' and Bigfoot. Zecharia Sitchin is the main source here, and another potential influence on Chris Boucher's formulation of Planet Five's history.

Zecharia's term for Planet Five was 'Tiamat' (after the goddess who stars in the Sumerian creation myth), and his hypothesis, expressed

---

[112] Asimov, Isaac, 'The Ultimate Crime', in *More Tales of the Black Widowers* (1976).

in his book: *The 12th Planet* (1976)[113] was that Sumerian myth contained 'precise and scientifically plausible cosmological concepts regarding the creation of our solar system'[114]:

> 'Furthest away was Tiamat. She was the "monster" that Marduk later shattered – the "missing planet." As the "missing planet", Tiamat was located beyond Mars.'

This is confusing, but by 'furthest' Sitchin means bounding the inner Solar System, as his scheme has Venus and Mars (Lahamu and Lahmu) coming into being between the inner bodies Apsu and Mummu (the Sun and Mercury) and the 'furthest' world, Tiamat (the trans-Martian 'missing planet')[115]. The Sumerians apparently snubbed Vulcan unmercifully and never mentioned it. Other planets come into being after Tiamat, and further out – Lahamu and Lahmu in their turn; Kistar (Jupiter), Anshar (Saturn), Gaga (Pluto – at that time next to Saturn), Anu (Uranus), and Nudimmid (Neptune).

Suddenly, Nudimmid (confusingly also Ea) attracts a giant rogue planet, Marduk; Marduk's passage creates the moons of Uranus, and disrupts Tiamat, tearing away 11 satellites, notably the chief Moon Kingu[116]; flings Gaga outwards; and finally tears Tiamat in two – one half forming the Earth, and the other the asteroid belt.

---

[113] Yes I know, we want to know about Planet Five, not Planet 12 – but bear with me.

[114] Zecharia Sitchin, *The 12th Planet* (Kindle edition), location 1415.

[115] Sitchin, *The 12th Planet*, location 3520.

[116] Later to become Earth's Moon – Sitchin is, perhaps, a real influence on Hogan's **Giants** novels.

The astronomer Patrick Moore (who once suggested to a pseudoscientist who believed in perfectly spherical Saturnians that 'they seemed to be extremely large balls'[117]) might well have asked Sitchin if his Solar System had ended up Gaga, but – despite the fact that this material only relates to astronomy in the very broadest sense – Sitchin was considered Russia's answer to Erich Von Däniken, and his work was well known in 1977 and sold, even in translation, in the millions.

Now I'm not suggesting Chris Boucher actually read Sitchin: for one thing, I've tried and it's heavy going. But the ideas of the book, the resurrection of Planet Five as something being talked about, and the idea that it (or some of it) could form the Earth, or come to Earth, was in the air.

A problem with the Tiamat account considered as astronomy[118] is, if half of Planet Five becomes the Earth and half the asteroid belt, why is the Earth so much more massive than all the bodies in the asteroid belt put together?

Where Did The Mass Go?

In *Image* there is a simple explanation for where the missing fifth planet went: it's still there. It exists in a time-loop, a temporal orbit, locked away from affecting the rest of the Solar System. While this relies on the established super-technology of the Time Lords rather than any possible human science, it is not implausible in those terms. The use of time-loops to seal off worlds considered

---

[117] It's unclear now how Moore got away with this remark on TV, but he recalls it in his book of talks, *Can You Speak Venusian? A Guide to the Independent Thinkers* (1972), p120.

[118] One of the problems.

dangerous from history was first shown in **Doctor Who** in *The War Games* (1969), where it was used to remove the world of the War Lords from the universe. The remaining mass now constituting the asteroid belt might be the remains of the Fifth Planet's moon.

By suggesting a dynamic, catastrophe-driven cosmology, the 'worlds in collision' model of the Solar System adapted by Sitchin, and popularised originally by Immanuel Velikowsky (*Worlds in Collision*, 1950), annoyed and alarmed astronomers at the time in equal measure. The preferred 'common model' was a gradual slow condensation of a nebula into an ordered planetary system, in which things stayed put where they'd been discovered and orbited nicely. While the bulk of the pseudoscience here is bunk, the position has shifted somewhat since.

The best (current) model for the formation of our Moon, for instance, is the Earth being hit a glancing blow by a wandering minor planet which essentially, knocked a Moon-sized lump out of the early Earth[119]. We now accept that the heavens may be violent. In 1977, the suggestion that planets like ours might break up, that evolution might end in a betrayal of all life rather than it climbing to some apotheosis, that we might be moving into a dead end – all formed disturbing and alienating ideas.

---

[119] This theory is called the Theia Impact, or 'the Big Splash', and the collision would have occurred about 4.5 billion years ago, well outside the timescale for *Image,* or even *The Silurians.*

Post-*Image* Theories, and Modern Fictional Usages: the Things *Image* May Have Influenced

Planet Five appears as Phaeton in Warren Ellis' graphic novel *Ocean* (2004)[120].

In *Ragnarok*, a rare, barely-animated 'video' of static drawings with a performed voiceover scripted by Alan Moore, that I watched around 1983 and which no one else in creation seems to have seen, a future space miner (based on prospector and gold-rush stereotypes with possibly even a robot mule, memory is starting to cheat) is digging in 'the shattered world' of the asteroid belt when he discovers a entombed telepathic tyrannosaur (the last survivor of Planet Five) which is then brought back to Earth and runs amok[121]. While a very minor work, I include it here because it's staggeringly good fun, and because it attributes to Planet Five a diabolical prehistoric entity (albeit one with a bigger head and small arms).

In his *Promethea* series dealing with Kabbalistic magic, Alan Moore uses the hole in the solar system made by the 'missing' Planet Five, to stand for the 'broken' circle of the sephiroth Daath, the one which leads to the 'back' of reality to the demons and inimical forces called qlippothic – which is to say, the illusionary side of

---

[120] Basically Ellis's version of Andrei Tarkovsky's 1972 film *Solaris*.

[121] The telepathic tyrannosaur makes a return appearance in Alan Moore's and Steve Bissette's comic **1963** #2 (Image Comics, 1993) with a different backstory, but it's still boasting of tearing the flying reptiles from the skies or cooking them (psychically) as they flew.

Malkuth experienced by adepts who refuse to give up their ego and become false Black Brothers[122] rather than progress[123].

In 2002 two NASA scientists revived the idea of the fifth planet (Planet V in their terminology), to provide a source for the material needed to explain the massive impact craters on the Moon, which date to the Late Heavy Bombardment Period of the Hadean Eon. Sadly for our desire to claim accuracy for **Doctor Who**, this new theory hasn't been widely accepted, and even if it were the lunar impacts date to between 3.8 and 4.1 billion BP, which is far earlier than a piddling 12 million years ago[124].

In 2015 a (probably!) spoof website announced that the former Soviet Republic of Tajikistan had claimed to have detected a fifth planet 250 million miles (402 million km) from Earth (sic) with an orbital period of five years, and were naming it 'Tajikistan'. The story was repeated (as being factual about Tajikistan's astronomy, if not about the fifth planet) by *Popular Mechanics*[125].

In 2015, the comics series *Nameless* by Grant Morrison depicted an asteroid on collision course with Earth, inhabited by an evil psychic force that may have been a god (or God!) from the remains of the fifth planet (unless it was all a dream in the mind of a military

---

[122] 'Evil' magicians in the only kabbalistic sense.

[123] Moore, Alan, JH Williams III and Mick Gray, **Promethea** #20 (2002).

[124] Chambers, JE and JJ Lissauer, 'A New Dynamical Model for the Lunar Late Heavy Bombardment', *Lunar and Planetary Science* #33, 2002.

[125] Wenz, John, 'According to Tajikistan, There's a New Fifth Planet From the Sun Called Tajikistan', *Popular Mechanics*, 2 September 2015.

psychic who'd failed to defeat something awful upon earth, or indeed something else — the jury's out until the last issue appears)[126].

It is clear that, in the popular psyche, the fifth planet is **now** associated with three things:

- Its destruction
- The consequent devastation of Mars
- One or more immensely mentally powerful monsters, with claims to Godhood.

The third one wasn't there before *Image*. The zeitgeist has spoken: **Doctor Who**, as is often the case, was there at the start. When we dream uneasily of the fifth planet now, we dream of the Fendahl — we just give it other names.

An Aside: What Happened to Mars? What Do the Doctor's Speculations in *Image* Tell Us? Is This Mere Carelessness? Will No-One Think of the Ice Warriors?

The Mars known to science in 1977 was far less hospitable as a possible home for life than that envisaged by earlier writers. Edgar Rice Burroughs, writing in the 1920s[127], could still make play with a Mars of canals, beautiful if oviparous Martian women, and societies with both swordplay and super-science, which was at least notionally contemporary with post-Civil War America, and which could be reached psychically if not physically.

---

[126] The last issue, #6, came out while I was proofing this archive. I am still unsure what in the story is real and what illusion, but its use of 'Marduk' for an outer planet suggests the influence of Sitchin.

[127] In his many sequels to *A Princess of Mars* (1917).

Later writers would displace this age of Mars to the past – most notably, Michael Moorcock in his **Kane of Old Mars** trilogy[128] – leading to the amusing bit in Alan Moore's second *League of Extraordinary Gentlemen*[129] series where the heroes of Burroughs' **Barsoom** novels and Edwin Lester Arnold's *Lieutenant Gulliver Jones: His Vacation* debate whether the historical Kane was a human transported to Mars (like them) or just a Martian with a human-sounding name. Others, like Ray Bradbury and Leigh Brackett, adopted a present Mars which preserved some of the past, but still projected a mythic golden age backward into ghostly glory[130]. Most of Brackett's Martian stories in fact have the same plot – something awful comes forward from the aeons-old history of Mars and has to be stopped[131].

As early as *The Ice Warriors* (1967) **Doctor Who** was hedging its bets by having its Martians found intact frozen in a glacier from the first Ice Age (sic). It's unclear whether this was meant to be thousands or millions of years before, but **Doctor Who** writers soon forgot this safety valve and contemporary Martians – though perhaps not from Mars any longer – were soon queuing up to invade Earth (*The Seeds of Death* (1969)), join and then betray the Galactic Federation (*Curse of Peladon* (1972) and *Monster of*

---

[128] Moorcock, Michael, *Warrior of Mars* (1965), *Blades of Mars* (1968), *Barbarians of Mars* (1969), collected in *Warrior of Mars* (1986).

[129] Moore, Alan, *The League of Extraordinary Gentlemen*, vol 2 #1 (2002), p7.

[130] Bradbury, Ray, *The Martian Chronicles* (1950).

[131] Brackett wrote many Martian short stories and novels, beginning with 'Martian Quest' for *Astounding Science Fiction* (February 1940).

Peladon (1974)), and – much later, though earliest of all in fictional chronology – pick up members of their terribly-prone-to-getting-frozen-in-ice race from Russian submarines (*Cold War* (2013)). Recently too, a form of life fought by the Ice Warrior Martians has been discovered in the form of intelligent water (*The Waters of Mars* (2009)). It's hard to see how any of that tallies with the Fendahl pausing to destroy all life on Mars 12 million years ago.

This whole theory is of course just an aside by the Doctor, and it's worth recalling that as recently as *The Android Invasion* he'd stated that his memory has been getting terribly bad, and that 300 years ago he'd have remembered the Kraal space-pods 'like a shot'[132]. It's also worth remembering that the Ice Warriors hadn't appeared on screen during the three-year span of the then-present Doctor.

The Devastation of Mars

We've seen how a substantial number of the earlier fictional uses for the 'explosion' theory of Planet Five had taken in a concomitant devastation of Mars, from Anne Elisa Smith, whose Mars is another battleground of the Deva, through WE Johns, whose Mars is brought low by the explosion of Kraka.

Indeed this idea of Mars having been laid waste or destroyed was so established in the popular idea of what constituted a science fiction novel that it appears even in satirical children's fiction. In Richmal Crompton's *William's Television Show* (1958), the 31st volume in her **Just William** series – in the story 'William Among The Chimney Pots' – a green-paint-splattered William poised on a roof inadvertently gives Professor Mayfield – who secretly also writes

---

[132] *The Android Invasion* episode 1.

science fiction for children[133] – much-needed inspiration for his next book:

> 'The green armour covering him from neck to toes. The green hands.'[134]

> 'A creature of supreme and evil intelligence...he has landed in Mars from some other planet and is laying it waste, exterminating the inhabitants or reducing them to a state of mechanical slavery. Those who land on Mars from our own planet escape only with their spirits broken and their bodies maimed. The book will be called *The Scourge of Mars*.'[135]

Why it's particularly in Chris Boucher's mind as a likely thing for the Doctor to say is that by 1977 we knew what the surface of Mars was like in far more detail. The early Russian landers had sent back limited information (and the Iron Curtain had potentially censored some of it), but the US 1976 Voyager 1 lander (landing on 20 July 1976) and its accompanying orbiter began a more substantial survey, sending back the first ever colour picture of the Martian

---

[133] 'His work as an economist won him the praise of the greatest intellects of his day, but […] appreciation of his space fiction gave him more pleasure than their most enthusiastic plaudits.' (Crompton, Richmal, *William's Television Show* (1958), p84.)

[134] Crompton, *William's Television Show*, p81. She writes these brief descriptions with such gusto, that it's tempting to imagine she'd have liked a crack at science fiction – and would have been good at it. In a few lines she covers the same ground as the Ice Warriors (green armour), the Fendahl (a supreme evil from another world), the Daleks (exterminating) and the Cybermen (reducing to mechanical slavery). If the story had been written after **Doctor Who**, the influence would have seemed irrefutable!

[135] Crompton, *William's Television Show*, p84.

surface (a long desert of red rusty rocks under a banded sky part pale blue, part pale red); an analysis of Martian soil; and the results of tests for organic molecules which were maddeningly inconclusive but which failed to prove the existence of life. Mars, it seemed, was a wasteland.

It was this image – the rocks, the dust, the empty cloudless sky – that would have displaced the Ice Warriors from any thinking about what **Doctor Who** might have previously implied about Mars. Indeed it is as if the Fendahl – escaping from a timeloop that somehow once **had** restrained it – devoured not just whatever lichens and anaerobic microbes might have seemed plausible in 1977, for a Mars of 12 million years before – but also all the baroque and impossible histories of Mars' past fictional epochs. It would take a (real) hiatus in the production of **Doctor Who**, and (within the fiction) both a Time War and a universal reboot[136], before the Ice Warriors would be seen again on screen.

---

[136] Respectively first mentioned in *Rose* (2005) and seen in *The Big Bang* (2010).

CHAPTER 5: THE BAD AND THE GOOD

We have already seen how *Image* uses Gothic trappings: the mist in the wood, the terror of the hiker, the Skull and the pentagram – in fact all the materials whose source may be traceable to *The Skull.* Around them it sets up a scientific investigation that, if uninterrupted by the Doctor and Leela, will lead to the rising of the Fendahl – but additionally, and rather sooner, to the destruction of the Earth. A marvel of science – the time scanner – is raised against the supernatural, just as in *Quatermass and the Pit* a dream-reading machine gives access to race memory of the Martians, or in *The Stone Tape* the science of recording determines the underlying physics of ghosts (as images replayed from a physical medium into the minds of the observers), but brings an almost greater danger of its own.

This mixture of Gothic and post-Gothic is what I think is the central strength of *Image* – but it is not by any means a perfect piece of drama. It has flaws, and some of them come close to fatally damaging it: only the multiple successes of good casting and cracking dialogue get the show past some of the following.

10 Flaws in Image[137]

1: What Exactly Does the Doctor Know about the Fendahl?

He identifies the Fendahleen as creatures from his own mythology. He knows enough about their mode of coming into being to suggest to Dr Fendelman that he X-rays Thea's skull, but he doesn't seem to know that they might be brought into being through a different skull. At least it's odd that if he knows the Skull is dangerous, he would he treat it as a prop for a soliloquy and offer it a jelly baby. Does he think it's sapient, or even sentient? Is it? We never actually hear what the Gallifreyan legend of the Fendahl consists of – except that it's death – but I think we have to assume the story has a skull in it somewhere. Just not necessarily a 12-million-year-old one.

2: How Far Away was the Fifth Planet from Earth?

107 million miles (172 million km) (television[138]), or 170 million miles (274 million km) (novelisation[139])? (Which is to say, 200 million miles (322 million km) or 267 million miles (430 million km) from the Sun?) The latter figure is within 10 million miles (16

---

[137] I'm not going to run the 'cheap and cheerful' defence here – I think these are all genuine mistakes or problems, and I think they could all have been fixed without in any way impacting the actual effectiveness (or even cost) of the work. However, the timescales and budgets of 1977's television production were – even relatively – less forgiving than those of today, and today's **Doctor Who** is still doing the impossible on budgets set for series in which you don't have to design new worlds or monsters every time, nor blow up quite so many things.

[138] Episode 3.

[139] Dicks, *Doctor Who and the Image of the Fendahl*, p74.

million km) of the average orbit of Ceres (from Earth), and to my mind fits better with Chris Boucher's track record of factual accuracy (Potassium-Argon dating, the palaeoarchaeological references, Kenya as the location of the Skull). Although Terrance Dicks' usual practice was (at this point) to work from videos – and he clearly does here because the novelisation includes the kiss on the cheek Leela gives Adam Colby, which both actors confirm in the DVD documentary was unscripted – it is tempting to think that either access to the original script, or a heads-up from Chris Boucher, here corrects a verbal slip on the part of the always amazing, but at times vocally peculiar, Tom Baker.

3: The Design of the Adult Fendahleen

I watched *Image* for this book several times myself, and re-watched it once with my wife Sarah and daughters Morgan (19) and Rhianna (16), to get the opinions of a once-mildly-interested viewer of 21st century **Who**, and two enthusiastic fans of it who have grown up with the post-2005 stories. In general they were very impressed, particularly with the atmospheric work in the first two episodes, and the level of drama built up between the supporting cast, for *Image* functions as a suspense thriller even without the Doctor's involvement. However, the moment when the large Fendahleen comes up the corridor simply triggered a massive collapse of their suspension of disbelief at the end of episode 3, and some sniggering.

This is, in part, of course due to modern special effects being better in some ways (although oddly, the laughably rubbish is seen just as much in bad CGI as it once was in bad physical effects) but it remains true that the basic Fendahleen, shot from the front, is (like

Alpha Centauri[140]) a creature that somewhat resembles a penis – and the standard **Doctor Who** solution for this, namely putting a cape on it, or a cobra hood arrangement at the sides, only conceals this so much.

The real problem though – for the similarly-designed embryonic Fendahleen are excellent – is that the poor man in the costume can only shuffle gradually forward from side to side, and while it doesn't matter that the monster only approaches slowly, which by episode 3 is a given, the clumsiness of its approach as well as its speed defuses any sense of menace. It really needed to glide slowly but uncannily, not waddle.

The small hissing Fendahleen which appear on the transforming bodies of victims are very much more effective than the full-scale one. Richmal Crompton's fictional science fiction writer Professor Mayfield (aka Martin Morrow) tells his illustrator:

> 'The things you've been doing are too large, too horrific[141]. Nothing large can be really sinister. To be really sinister the creature must be small. Smallness is the essence of the sinister, and green is the essential colour of the sinister.'[142]

I'm inclined to agree with him/her.

---

[140] In *The Curse of Peladon* and *The Monster of Peladon*.
[141] Perhaps they also looked too much like a penis, but in 1958 Richmal Crompton couldn't have her professor tell his illustrator that in a children's book.
[142] Crompton, *William's Television Show* , p81.

4: The Clashing Threats of the Time Scanner and the Fendahl

A line to the effect that the Fendahl will absorb the explosion and grow ever stronger would defuse the possibility that just waiting would end its threat to the universe (with the relative disadvantage of course of having destroyed Earth). As it is, this is where the two threats fail to collide but sort of sidle past each other with a tight smile and a small nod of the head. The sheer amount of jeopardy conceals the fact that to win the Doctor just has to turn a machine off, and put a skull in a box.

5: What's Max Stael's Motivation, Darling?

I mean obviously he wants power: he'd like people to worship him, and he probably enjoys some intense grovelling if he can get it from 'meddling fools'[143] – but he's a personable chap, must be paid a fair amount by Fendelman: he could probably just hire some worshippers, or start a cult in a city where there are nicer-looking acolytes than Ted Moss (no offence to Ted). He's clearly misunderstood the relationship he'll be in with the forces he's summoning – he thinks 'master', the reality will be 'food' – but it would help if we had some sense of what his Stael Utopia might be, or what need drives him. It's possible to imagine a subtext that places him in a triangle where Adam fancies Thea (the kiss on the hand in scene one), Thea fancies Max (the occasional glance, her intonation of 'Max, don't be such a fool', after he's left her tied up[144]) and Max just wants Adam to get on his knees ('It depends on whether I enjoy having you worship me'[145]), but that might be a

---

[143] Episode 2.

[144] Episode 2.

[145] Episode 3.

step too far. Still, we can forgive this for the wonderful creepiness of his performance and his nicely underplayed suicide, once he's realized that he's just going to become part of something greater and more horrible than ever he expected.

6: How do people Know What They Know?

How does Fendelman know that the creature is called the Fendahl? He comes in after the Doctor has used the term 'Fendahleen', and after the vision of the creatures has faded. He knows the Doctor has queried his name, but how does he know that shows the name of the creature? His speech about how he, and all his forefathers, have been used is well delivered, but logically it's a huge leap. (For that matter, why **is** it called the Fendahl – what does the name mean, and who called it that? The dying people it fed off on Planet Five? The Time Lords horrified by what they found there?) The Doctor mentions 'the superstitions of this planet' but I can't find any[146]. How does the Doctor know the guard is called Mitchell, and that the other dead body was a hiker? He might know the guard's name if he was listening just outside the door when Adam and Thea are discussing the death, but why would he be?

7: Who lets the Doctor out of the Store Cupboard?

The obvious suspects are Adam or Thea, because they're the most open-minded and the most likely to want to hear what he actually has to say. Unfortunately the episode is cut so that immediately after the lock clicks open Adam and Thea are shown entering Fendelman's lab together in mid-argument, which visually suggests

---

[146] Episode 4. In context he may mean that the tradition of 13 witches to a coven may derive from 12 Fendahleen and a Core, rather than there being a human legend of the Fendahl as such.

it wasn't them (at least not singly, and if it they were in cahoots we'd expect them to comment on it at some later point.) It could, physically, have been Max, but why would he? And he doesn't seem concerned either way when Ted is trying to warn him of investigators.

Now of course, looking back from 21st-century **Doctor Who**, we can imagine an intervention from Clara in the Doctor's past (like those seen in *The Time of the Doctor* (2013), or his ability to telepathically get a wooden door to open (as shown in *Heaven Sent* (2015)), but such retrospective fixes don't prevent the problem existing in the first place.

8: If Max Knows as Much about the Fendahl as he Later Seems to, Why Is He So Horrified By The Manner Of The Hiker's Death?

Is he just overacting, because he thinks people will expect him to be horrified? If so, he shouldn't bother – nobody pays him any attention. He later speaks to Ted of leaving 'a place for the one who kills', so he appears to have been expecting to have summoned something lethal – was he just expecting it to come when called, rather than suddenly crop up on its own timetable?

9: The Shining

This one may not be a flaw – it might be a simple ingenious touch that alters the whole way you look at *Image*, in fact I'm not sure that I haven't just invented it – but doesn't it strike you as odd that even for a moment, even in the first faint beginning of the effect, no one ever shouts: 'Hey come and look at this Skull, it's only bloody **glowing**!'?

In other words, how much of what we see, when we the audience see the Skull begin to glow, is intended to be a diegetic 'physical event' in the world of the episode –something that could be, in theory, recorded by a closed-circuit TV camera if Fendelman had set one up? How much of it is (what might be termed) 'telediegetic' – the audience seeing through the eyes of the person the Skull's power is influencing, as they see it glow at the time but can't tell anyone afterwards because it affects their memory? And how much is non-diegetic – we see it to give an impression of what it would feel like, but it's not intended to be actually how it would have looked, but rather a symbolic representation of it[147]?

Is the glow an illusion, or are we seeing the Skull in the-world-as-depicted generating real photons? If you tried to read a book you didn't know by the Skull's light, would you see the real text, or just a hymn to the Fendahl? I wish I knew, and I wish I could believe the production team and the author had meant anything other than that it's really glowing – I just think it's odd that no one ever manages to say that it was.

10: What Did the Time Loop Do?

If a Time Loop also removes all records of a thing time looped, why does the Doctor remember being terrified by Time Lord stories of the Fendahl as a child and why are there still Earth legends of it? (That said, Gallifrey exists in a special relationship to time[148], and I

---

[147] Just as romantic music symbolises falling in love in certain rom-coms, but we aren't necessarily expected to think love really feels like 'Ah! Sweet Mystery of Life' playing in Millie's head in *Thoroughly Modern Millie* (1967) (although we can if we like).

[148] 'I'm more from what you might call Inner Time.' (*The Stones of Blood* (1978)).

couldn't find any legends.) Why would a time loop affect Time Lord records? You'd think they'd keep their records outside time[149].

Six Top Things About *Image*, (including one top thing about its director)[150]

There are, though, also plenty of good things about *Image* that I've only had time to hint at – here are some aspects of it that more than outweigh the above flaws.

1: The Way It Transcends the Comedy Yokel

Doctor Who has a patchy record of being fair to people living in the countryside even if they're not Welsh or Scottish, often seeming to view them with a mixture of dismissal and fear. They'll either be unable to ride a bicycle and muttering to themselves in mock Zummerset / sub-Stanley Unwin nonsense (yes Pigbin Josh, we mean you – I know you now have an ironic following, but really what was Barry Letts thinking when he let that bit of *The Claws Of Axos* (1971) get filmed?), or as per **K9 and Company**: *A Girls' Best Friend* (1981) or *The Dæmons* they'll be happy cannon-fodder to the first local cult that asks them to sacrifice incomers to Hecate or Azal. This view of the countryside wasn't left in the 1970s, and isn't

---

[149] This is actually, if I've understood it, a plot-point in an audio drama in Big Finish Productions', **Gallifrey** series, *The Inquiry* (2004), where records in the Time Lord Matrix are unchanged by an alteration in time. (See also the footnotes to Appendix 2.)

[150] The heights are much higher than the troughs are low – this is a story that mainly works – and its verve and sense of danger carry it past many minor flaws. Throughout this analysis I've looked at the pre-eminent place I believe *Image* holds in all pre-2005 **Doctor Who**, as a truly modern work of horror. I'm not going to rehash that here – instead, these are four other brilliant things about it.

limited to **Doctor Who** – it's all through the modern series **The Midsomer Murders** for instance, where moving to the country is a sure sign of incipient death, and at least one person per episode – even if not the murderer – will prove to be part of a cult, wife-swapping circle or at least a monomaniac group of bell-ringers, brass-rubbers, or 1970s revivalists[151].

Image knowingly flirts with the latter stereotype, but pretty soon is making joyous comedy out of it and turning lots of its basic assumptions on its head. Ted Moss is a suspicious (and superstitious) yokel, cutting hedges for the council and carrying a mysterious charm, and as we see later he's part of Max's coven – but he's also thoroughly cowed and under the thumb of the impressive local witch and matriarch Mother Tyler, who with her son Jack forms the cavalry that pulls the Doctor and Leela's chestnuts out of the fire several times in the course of *Image* (if you'll excuse my mixed metaphor). From the moment in episode 1 when Mother Tyler stares down the pseudo-cockney security guard Mitchell who's threatened to set his dog on her, with the lines:

> 'Don't 'ee mind him, my lovelies. Sooner or later he'll be sorry. Later or sooner, he'll regret. Well, I'll be going now, Professor. You can tell Doctor Fendelman I'll come back when the others is gone. I don't hold with the likes of 'ee.

---

[151] The season 10 episode *Dance with the Dead* by Peter J Hammond, which aired first on 12 November 2006, is set in the Midsomer village of 'Morton Fendle'. Ironically this is one of the few **Midsomer Murders** episodes in which a body is not found by someone walking their dog.

Hm. There isn't a dog born as'd attack me, boy. They got more sense than most people.[152]'

…we know we're in for a treat whenever she's on screen.

I particularly like too, the sequence in episode 4, after the Fendahleen has been dispatched by salt, in which Martha Tyler tells her son Jack (who is putting a companionable arm around her shoulder): 'You know summat, John? There's going a come a time when I'll be too old for this sort of thing.'[153] This is very effective because the sentiment is a cliché, and one that we now associate with the speech the older cop makes to the rookie officer in a traditional New York precinct police drama (due, of course, to its later, slightly more scatological appearance as Danny Glover's catchphrase in the **Lethal Weapon** films). By 1977 it had already appeared in **Doctor Who** ('Oh I'm getting too old for this sort of thing – it's ridiculous' (The Monk, 'Checkmate' (*The Time Meddler* episode 4, 1965))), *The Godfather*, Disney's *Robin Hood*, and *Star Wars* (25 May 1977) as Obi-Wan's persuasive plea to Luke (uttered disarmingly and disingenuously rather than as a witticism) that 'I'm getting too old for this sort of thing'.

With Mother Tyler it is subverted firstly because despite her age, she won't admit that she's **already** reached such a point, just that it might one day happen, and secondly her phrasing strongly implies that killing monsters with rock salt is par for the course for her, if not old hat.

---

[152] Episode 1.
[153] Episode 4.

Given **Doctor Who** fandom's appreciation of the 'Holmesian double-act' – supporting characters who enliven a piece with their banter and asides, referring most notably to the partnership between Doctor Litefoot and Henry Jago in Robert Holmes' *Talons of Weng-Chiang* – it is a shame that enough kudos hasn't been given to the pure fun of the Martha and Jack Tyler duo.

Here's one last example: Martha explaining to her grandson why she doesn't trust the Doctor.

MARTHA

I didn't reckon he'd be reliable. Never trust a man as wears a hat.

JACK

Well, Granddad always wore one.

MARTHA

And a wicked old devil he were, too.

JACK

Well, I wear one.

MARTHA

Ah, but I give it to 'ee. That's different.[154]

2: The Smile on the Face of the Tiger

In the first scene of *Image* Adam tells Max: 'end the day with a smile' – but though he literally ends that day with one, he won't be smiling at the end of his days. The creature that Thea becomes will,

---

[154] Episode 2.

however, smile. The bland self-satisfied emptiness of the smile Thea gives as she ascends in the form of the Fendahl is serendipitously effective[155]. The DVD cast documentary makes it clear that Wanda Ventham (Thea), unable to see with her eyelids shut and painted as staring eyes[156], found her facial expressions hard to manage. By chance her smile is supremely eerie, being an inhuman, wordless, satisfaction – a transcendent smugness, that suggests mindless omnipotence, a vacuous grin behind which nothing conscious (as we understand consciousness) exists.

3: How the Doctor Brings Mother Tyler Back from the Brink

The cake! The pleasure here – and it's one modern **Who** has set aside in favour of the different pleasure of having a fish-out-of-water Doctor who doesn't understand humanity through and through – is that this method of bringing Mother Tyler back from the darkness of the soul the image of the Fendahl has cast across her spirit, can only work because the Doctor is wise and knows us and thoroughly understands the strengths and weaknesses of humanity. Having sent Jack Tyler off to get the tea:

---

[155] Episode 4, at 3m16s – just after she's converted two of the coven into Fendahleen.

[156] This, too, I find to be strangely effective. The Fendahl is not like a living thing at all, its eyes are painted like a Greek statue's. It doesn't threaten, or harangue or boast – like the Medusa it looks and changes its victims, but it turns them not to statues but to subservient parts of itself. Stephan Moffat was 16 when *Image* was broadcast – I wonder if his Weeping Angels have a root here. Like them, the Thea-as-Fendahl is statue-like, seemingly blind, beautiful and deadly.

DOCTOR

Off you go. Make some. Use the best china, four cups, lay it out on a tray, off you go. Oh! And some fruit cake.

JACK

Anything else?

DOCTOR

No.

ASIDE TO LEELA

I love fruitcake.

SHOUTING

Come on, Mrs Tyler. This is no way to behave when you've got visitors. We've come for tea!

LEELA

And fruitcake.

DOCTOR

And fruitca...

A cutaway to Fendelman's lab follows, then back to the cottage:

DOCTOR [OFF CAMERA]

Then you mix the peanuts with the treacle

JACK ENTERS WITH THE TEA TRAY, AS ORDERED

DOCTOR

Throw in the apple cores very hard, put the lot in a shallow tin and bake in a high oven for two weeks.

SOTTO VOCE

It's too late. She's slipping away. Come on.

MARTHA

Here, just a minute.

DOCTOR

What is it?

MARTHA

That ain't the way to make a fruitcake![157]

4: The Human Drama between the Main Characters

Can Fendelman tempt Colby into not reporting the dead hiker to the police? What is Stael really up to? And what is the real relationship between Adam and Thea?

FENDELMAN

Adam, Adam, just think for a moment. These woods, they are supposed to be haunted. Now, can you imagine what would happen if there were news of a mysterious death in them?

---

[157] Episode 2.

THEA

Well, there'd be a certain amount of publicity.

FENDELMAN

Publicity? It would be a circus. They attract enough lunatics already without advertising for them.

COLBY

Well, I don't see that we've much alternative.

FENDELMAN

Adam, Adam. Our work is at a critical stage. Your discovery could be one of the most important milestones in human development. Your work will fundamentally affect how man views himself. We cannot be interrupted at this moment of destiny.

COLBY

Yes, but –

FENDELMAN

And besides, we wouldn't want your Nobel Prize to be jeopardised by an unfortunate coincidence, now would we?[158]

Before the real horror sweeps over them, there's a genuine **Thirty-Minute Theatre / Play for the Day** feel about the acting and realism of this story. That was the main thing to impress my

---

[158] Episode 1.

116

children as to the difference in tone from the **Doctor Who** of the last 11 years.

5. Its Legacy of Names

Not something its original audience could enjoy, but now as we watch in retrospect, the likely origins of some of Russell T Davies's favourite character names shine out from Chris Boucher's choices: Tyler, Martha, Jack, Adam. While Davies writes that he chose Rose as 'the most English of names', perhaps another part of him was choosing 'Tyler' as one of the most **Who**ish[159].

6. Interesting Facts about the Director of *Image*

George Spenton-Foster began work as an associate producer for the BBC on – among other things – dramatic adaptations of science fiction stories for **Out Of The Unknown** including adaptions of the short stories: 'The World In Silence' by John Rankine, 'Lambda 1' by Colin Kapp, 'Some Lapse of Time' by John Brunner, and 'The Counterfeit Man' by Alan Nourse. On *The World In Silence* (1966) he worked with Deborah Watling, who would go on to join the cast of **Doctor Who**.

He went on to produce anthology shows such as **The Man Outside** (1972) and **Thirty-Minute Theatre** (1965-73) which often had a fantasy or science fiction component; he most notable episode (in terms of resemblance to **Doctor Who**) being *The Metal Martyr* (from a story by Robert Moore Williams), dramatised by Derrick Sherwin and designed by Raymond Cusick:

---

[159] Davies, Russell T, and Benjamin Cook, *The Writer's Tale: The Final Chapter*, p41.

'The robots have rebelled against man and now they are the rulers until one day Robot Two has a new thought – he thinks that he is a man. His thought is to have far-reaching consequences for mankind, who through him learn something of their rich heritage.'[160]

If *The Metal Martyr* still existed (of **Thirty-Minute Theatre**'s 286 episodes, over 230 are believed to be lost), it would cast light on how the BBC might have realised the script *The Masters of Luxor* by Anthony Coburn, which almost became **Doctor Who**'s second story – and which would have required designer Raymond Cusick to work on similar humanoid robots.

After *Image* George Spenton-Foster he would direct *The Ribos Operation* (1978) for Doctor Who and episodes of **Survivors** (1975-77) – and the **Blake's 7** episodes *Pressure Point*, *Voice From The Past*, *Weapon* and *Gambit* (all 1979).

---

[160] *Radio Times*, 23 to 29 December 1967.

APPENDIX 1: AFTERIMAGE OF THE FENDAHL

Doctor Who and the Image of the Fendahl (1979) by Terrance Dicks

Any adaption of a work into a different medium is itself a critique of the original work. In the case of novelisations, what the noveliser chooses to emphasise, reorder, conceal, or change shows his or her opinion of the original. As in all his novelisations of **Doctor Who** stories – and indeed his own work for children – Terrance Dicks writes clean and easily-read prose, although I can't help but feel his description of Max Stael is overstating the point when it uses 'stiff' and 'Germanic' twice each in one sentence, immediately after 'Prussian' in the one before:

> 'The lab door was flung open and Max Stael appeared, looking round the untidy laboratory with distaste, like a Prussian Officer on the parade ground. His stiff Germanic good looks reflected his stiff Germanic character.'[161]

It's a wonder he didn't click his heels and exit with a 'Ja wohl'.

There are some minor corrections in the novelisation of things which Terrance Dicks felt either didn't work or were wrong on screen. We see him doing this even in later novelisations and novels – his first novel for BBC Enterprises, *The Eight Doctors*

---

[161] Dicks, *Doctor Who and the Image of the Fendahl*, p9.

(1997), sees him putting the boot into *Doctor Who* (1996) for example[162].

Among his changes to *Image* as seen on television are:

- The move of the hiker's death to the first scene, and the replacement of the hiker's whistling of 'The Entertainer' with a mental recitation of part of *The Rime of the Ancient Mariner*. Alan Barnes mentions this is misquoted[163], but the misquotation is part of Terrance Dicks' characterisation of the hiker: 'How did it go? [...] Something like that anyway.'[164]

- The restatement of the distance to the fifth planet from 107 million miles to 170 million miles, which tallies better with the real-world distance of Ceres[165].

- A change to how the Doctor escapes from the locked room. In the television version, this is an unresolved plot point – someone releases him, but who and why is lost in the shuffle. In the novelisation, the Doctor gets so cross he breaks the lock:

    'The Doctor gave the door a hearty kick. There was a tinkle of shattered metal, and it swung open. He must have weakened some vital part of the lock after all, and the kick had done the rest.'

---

[162] '...a weird, fantastic adventure, full of improbable, illogical events' (Dicks, Terrance, *The Eight Doctors* p1).
[163] Barnes, 'The Fact of Fiction'.
[164] P7.
[165] P74.

This extends the joke from the preceding scene of Leela telling Jack that the Doctor 'has great knowledge. And a kind of – gentleness...'[166]

- The novelisation fills in Max Stael's unhappy childhood in a few telling lines, and explains how he has come to create his own religion, and that his aim is power[167].

The Taking of Planet 5 (1999) by Simon Bucher-Jones and Mark Clapham

In this tie-in novel, published by BBC Enterprises, no Fendahl actually appear, but in a further twist of the evolutionary history of Planet 5, within an accelerating time spiral (a variation of the time loop set up by the Time Lords to create weapons for their time war[168]), something evolves that acts as a predator upon the Fendahl. Like the Fendahl itself, this entity is ultimately the end result of 'human' evolution.

I asked one of the authors (Simon Bucher-Jones, that is, me) in a private interview, what he liked about *Image*. Recursively he referred me to this whole book as his answer. Pressed as to why he had drawn on *Image* in *The Taking of Planet 5* he commented:

'I was looking for dreadful things the war could have forced the Time Lords to do, and it seemed to me that releasing the Fendahl would be such a thing – and then I wondered what

---

[166] P48.

[167] Pp64-68.

[168] Not the Time War of the 21st-century TV series, but an earlier conflict specific to the eighth Doctor novels.

would have occurred if they'd tried to work the Fendahl's own trick on itself – to hijack its evolution.'

In *The Taking of Planet 5*, the planet is referred to in the display in Professor Mileo Twistnedine's Wandering Museum of The Verifiably Phantasmagoric, by the name Thyrop-Minerva – a deliberate reference by the author to the works of both Brian Lumley and James P Hogan. However, it is never stated that this is its real name, and the museum's status as 'The Museum of Things That Don't Exist' would suggest that the name is apocryphal, rather than the name the world would have 'really' been given by its inhabitants.

The Kaldor City Audios (2001-04)

These were a marvellous series of audios developing, under licence, the characters from Chris Boucher's **Doctor Who** and **Blake's 7** stories, and mainly starring a character played by Paul Darrow, known here as Kaston Iago, who may or may not be a post-**Blake's 7** Kerr Avon.

They begin with the finding of a skull, in the great desert outside Kaldor City from *The Robots of Death*, which is purported to be that of the homicidal self-styled leader of the robots, Taren Kapel. Without spoiling these here, it is sufficient to say that we start with Scott Fredericks (Stael in *Image*) reprising his role of Carnell from the **Blake's 7** episode *Weapon* (1979), and we end with the understanding that he has gradually as Carnell (or perhaps always) been fulfilling the function once enacted by Max Stael. In the final audio to date (and the position reached, and the sad death of actor Russell Hunter, who brilliantly reprises his role as Uvanov in *The Robots of Death* in the audios, probably preclude any further work in the series) we maybe get to see the subjective experience of being inside what might be termed the Fendahl Singularity.

There have also been short stories and a stage play set in this continuity, including a planned stage version of *Image of the Fendahl* in Manchester in 2016, using **Kaldor City** audio characters in place of the Doctor and Leela[169].

Deus Le Volt (2006) by Jon de Burgh Miller

In this novella in the spin-off **Time Hunter** series, we get to see how the cult that comes into being around the Fendahl rationalises its worship. At least at the time of the Crusades they see it as 'a beast of unimaginable power, From the Book of Revelation itself'. Although 'Few survive its presence', to be killed by it is to 'live for eternity in paradise… [to] rule over the firmament, seated at the right hand of the new ruler of Heaven'. Their worship centres round 'a large fragment of bone.'[170] This – believed by the cult to be the spear that pierced Christ's side (generally known in occult fiction as the Spear of Longinus) – is marked with a pentagram. This is a slightly bathetic image and worryingly suggests that the Fendahl left a whole skeleton on earth, every bit of which has its energy running through it in a pentagram-shaped circuit like a sort of psionic Blackpool rock. So dreadful is the possibility of the Fendahl's manifestation in 1098 that forces from the far future return to this time, and its predestined comeuppance is once more restored to the 20th century (implicitly, to the events of *Image*).

---

[169] Stevens, Alan, personal correspondence with the editor.

[170] De Burgh Miller, Jon, *Time Hunter: Deus Le Volt* (2006), pp14-15.

APPENDIX 2: AN UNSUPPORTED FAN THEORY

What if the real name of Planet Five, never stated in *Image*, was nevertheless revealed to us in another **Doctor Who** story in that season?

I'd like you to consider for a moment the following 'facts'.

All the season 15 stories before *Underworld* are set around or in the Solar System – a history is being built up as Leela is being educated about her ancestors (whom she's getting sick of the Doctor going on about). After *Horror of Fang Rock*, which is an Edwardian story tonally similar to *The Talons of Weng-Chiang*, we are shown *The Invisible Enemy* – humanity preparing to leave the Solar System in the Great Break-Out of 5000 AD; *Image* – a look back at humanity's evolution and the past of the Solar System; and *The Sun Makers* – an account of the Solar System's future and humankind's sojourns on Mars and then Pluto, after the end of Old Earth. Tonally, to that point, it's a post-Gothic season, with a through focus on humanity's fictional history.

Then, in *Underworld*, it presents the audience with events at the edge of the universe, involving a humanoid race in an unknown time from a world never mentioned before, whose culture echoes Greek Myth. If there is no connection with humanity, this is a substantial sheer away from the feeling of the season up to that point.

The aliens we know to have originated in the relative proximity of Earth (and its Solar System) are all, even if bipedal, inhuman (that is although bipedal they could not pass as human) or alien. Mars has

Ice Warriors, Alpha Centauri has hermaphroditic hexapods, Arcturus has wizened things in mobile tanks. Draconians are clearly not descended from a common ancestor with apes. Even Earth's previous cycles of evolution had Silurians and Sea Devils rather than 'humans'.

Although we tend to think of aliens in **Doctor Who** as being often 'humanoid', the numbers of species that are both indistinguishable from and unconnected to Earth humans is actually quite small.

Skaro has humanoids that could pass for humankind, but they may have evolved from human ancestors taken there in prehistory (at least according to Terry Nation's then-recent *Radio Times* short story 'We Are the Daleks!', which *Genesis of the Daleks* neither confirms nor denies, despite having an opportunity to do so). When the Doctor and Harry's scans are examined by Ronson, humans are found to be essentially the same as Kaleds with a few minor differences, while the Doctor (internally) is quite different[171]. The Morestrans of *Planet of Evil* may be descendants of mankind[172], recognizing as they do that Tellus has been abandoned in the past.

---

[171] In the novelisation, at least. Ronson's 'Nothing conforms to any known life on this planet, apart from external appearances' (*Genesis of the Daleks* episode 2) doesn't make it clear if he is referring only to the Doctor, or both him and Harry. The novelisation, *Doctor Who and the Genesis of the Daleks* by Terrance Dicks, draws a distinction:

> "'**His** makeup,' he nodded toward Harry, 'is comparable to ours, with a few minor differences. But yours... nothing conforms to any known life form on this planet. **Nothing** – except the external appearance."' (p41).

[172] The Doctor and Sarah are '30,000 years' too late for Earth (*Planet of Evil* episode one). It's more likely than not that

Apart from the Time Lords – whose resemblance to humanity is a given – up to the transmission of *Underworld* in January 1978 there had been **no** aliens that could pass for human (with no possible connection to humanity) for the whole of Tom Baker's run – a period then of four years. Going back further to *Carnival of Monsters* (1973), we find the Lurmans Vorg and Shirna coded as a satirical/comedic pair of extraterrestrial carny-folk rather than a species. Arguably the last seriously-depicted alien race to resemble humanity was that of the War Lord, as far back as 1969.

Because **Doctor Who** has, as well as the fannish audience who keep watching, a churn of audience members as children watch and then perhaps drift away in their teen years, there will have been an (albeit unconscious) expectation in a lot of the audience that the human appearance of the Minyans must code them as being in some way our kin.

There were really only two human-like worlds in **Doctor Who** which had been established by 1978 as existing in the past and having been destroyed: the recently referenced Planet Five, and Minyos.

Minyos – the world which we learn of in *Underworld* – perished in a war fought as a result of Time Lord intervention in their

---

Morestrans are Earth–descended, as their names are human ones. It's true they use 'earthling' and 'alien' to denote Sarah, but they seem to use 'earthling' to mean any oxygen-user, and she finds their ship's atmosphere perfectly breathable once the hold is oxygenated. By 'alien' they may mean to their particular society. They don't seem surprised that someone might come from Earth, except insofar that Zeta Minor is so remote, and they speak in terms of saving their 'civilisation', not their species.

development. But what if Minyos and Planet Five were one and the same?

The searchers of the R1C have been looking for the P7E for 100,000 years[173]. They recognize the sound of the TARDIS as a 'reality dimensional stabilizer in materialisation phase as used in [...] the timeships of the Gods.' The Time Lords tried to help the Minyans when they 'were new at time-space exploration' – but they were 'kicked [...] out at gunpoint' by the Minyans, who 'went to war with each other, learned how to split the atom, discovered the toothbrush, and finally split the planet'[174].

The audience is left to make the assumption that the splitting of the planet results from the splitting of the atom – as with Lucifer in Heinlein's *Space Cadet* – but perhaps it results from experiments with time weapons[175]? Could the end of Minyos, and the conditions

---

[173] The ageing of their machinery indicates this, and the Doctor says 'The Minyan civilisation was destroyed a hundred thousand years ago on the other side of the universe' (*Underworld* episode one) – but since we don't know where we are (they've got as far as a coalescing spiral nebula on what is either the edge of space-time, the edge of the local group of galaxies or the edge of our galaxy, any of which is a long way away – especially with an ion drive, which is generally coded in SF as working at sublight speeds), or what the date is in Earth time 'now', this doesn't prevent Minyos and Planet Five being connected. (It is also possible that they have been travelling near light-speed for a subjective 100,000 years, and have in fact been searching for a substantially longer period of time when measured in a non-accelerated framework.)

[174] *Underworld* episode one.

[175] According to the Big Finish audio *The Inquiry*, Minyos is destroyed by a so-called 'Timonic Fusion Device', accidentally lost from Gallifrey's future. So confused are the politics and time

that sent evolution into a dead-end on Planet Five, have been the consequence of temporal weaponry? Perhaps an attempt to alter the Minyans' own past?

We know that 'Time Lords transcended such primitive mechanical techniques [as intercepting a transmat beam] when the universe was less than half its present size'[176]. We may presume their time-travel capability and their 'new' space-time exploration dates to the same period. Later in 'The Ultimate Foe' (*The Trial of a Time Lord* episodes 13-14) we are assured that the Time Lords have had '10 million years of absolute power'[177]. How likely is it that a time travelling race's first 'new' actions with space-time exploration took place either billions or millions of years in their relative future[178]? Wouldn't they first explore the near past and the near future? (Indeed some stories suggest that the Gallifreyan noosphere has its limits and TARDISes can't go too far into 'their' future[179].) It seems to me likely that *Underworld* does not take place in 1977, and that while the destruction of Minyos is 100,000 years ago in the subjective experience of the Minyan crew of the R1C, this says

---

mechanics involved, however, that the events are not definitive, and the 'accident' could have been deliberately arranged.

[176] *Genesis of the Daleks* episode one.

[177] *The Trial of a Time Lord* episode 13.

[178] If *Genesis of the Daleks* takes place a few thousand years before *The Dalek Invasion of Earth*, as *Planet of the Daleks* suggests, and the universe has expanded (apart from during the inflationary period) at essentially the same speed for roughly 13.7 billion years, the Time Lord's 'half its present size' is roughly 6.6 billion years on that scale – assuming he wasn't indulging in hyperbole.

[179] *Frontios* (1984).

nothing about when (relative to Earth or Gallifrey) that destruction was.

Assuming the lowest level of 'absolute' Gallifreyan mastery, the sixth Doctor's '10 million' years is not dissimilar to the 12 million between the Fendahl's era and 1977. A test of the time-travel facility by sending explorers two million years back into the past of an interesting Solar System[180] seems intuitively more likely than a wild flight of nine million years or more into Gallifrey's relative future. If the longer time-scale for Gallifreyan power is applied, the argument becomes even more convincing.

Perhaps the nuclear destruction of Minyos was even a first intervention – before the even more dreadful step of time-looping the Planet – to prevent the evolution of the Fendahl?

Was the Skull Adam Colby found in Kenya the skull of a human inhabitant of Minyos? Would Robert Holmes as script editor have made that connection? It is very tempting. (I think so anyway.)

And maybe there's even a wilder hypothesis – suppose the Time Lords tried to help the Minyans, but the Minyans seized time weapons. Suppose a renegade Time Lord helped them, and they schemed to invade other worlds to create a great and unstoppable army. Suppose they were time-looped, but because the loop was part of the Time Lord's own history it went wrong. It became a

---

[180] An even more sinister idea occurs – suppose you wanted to publicly display your mastery over time, wouldn't detonating a world or a sun, two million light years away, two million years ago – so that the sight of its destruction is detectable at once, at home – make a very nice firework display? How far away is Gallifrey from Earth again?

time-spiral, which cycled and recycled evolution, until it became the Fendahl, and for the first time in history a single world had to be timelooped twice because it had birthed both War Lords and monsters. Is this the history of our ancestors? War and Gods? Perhaps, and yet Minyos also birthed the hopeful questers of the P7E, and which in the end would we want to have as our heritage?

Thank you for reading.

BIBLIOGRAPHY

Books

Aldiss, Brian, with David Wingrove, *Trillion Year Spree: The History of Science Fiction*. Updated version of *Billion Year Spree: The History of Science Fiction*, 1973. London, Grafton Books, 1988. ISBN 9780586086841.

Arnold, EL, *Lieut Gullivar Jones: His Vacation*. London, SC Brown, Langham and Co, 1905.

Asimov, Isaac, *I, Robot*. 1950. London, Granada Publishing, 1968. ISBN 9780586025321.

Asimov, Isaac, *The Caves of Steel*. 1954. London, Granada Publishing, 1958. ISBN 9780586008355.

Asimov, Isaac, *The Naked Sun*. 1957. London, Granada Publishing, 1960. ISBN 9780586010167.

Asimov, Isaac, *More Tales of the Black Widowers*. 1976. London, Granada Publishing, 1980. ISBN 9780586047880.

Asimov, Isaac, Charles G Waugh and Martin H Greenberg, *The Mammoth Book of Golden Age SF*. London, Robinson Publishing, 2007. ISBN 9781845290962.

Austen, Jane, *Northanger Abbey*. 1818. Knoxville TN, Wordsworth Classics edition, 2007. ISBN 9781853260438.

Beckford, William, *Vathek*. London, J Johnson, 1786.

Berry, Arthur, *A Short History of Astronomy*. 1898. Kindle edition. Ulan Press, 2012. ASIN B009YPPNJA.

Birch Dinah, *The Oxford Companion To English Literature*. Seventh edition. Oxford, Oxford University Press, 2009. ISBN 9780192806871.

Bloch, Robert, *The Complete Stories of Robert Bloch Volume 1: Final Reckonings*. New York City, Carole Publishing Group, 1990. ISBN 9780806511443.

Bradbury, Ray, *The Martian Chronicles*. New York, Doubleday, 1950. ISBN 9780385038621.

Bronowski, J, *The Ascent of Man*. Boston, Little Brown & Co, 1974. ISBN 9780316109307.

Bucher-Jones, Simon, *Ghost Devices*. **The New Adventures**. London, Virgin Publishing Ltd, 1997. ISBN 9780426205142.

Bucher-Jones, Simon, and Mark Clapham M, *The Taking of Planet 5*. **Doctor Who: The Eighth Doctor Adventures**. London, BBC Books, 1999. ISBN 9780563555858.

Burroughs, Edgar Rice, *A Princess of Mars*. Chicago, AC McClurg, 1917.

Čapek, Karel *RUR*. 1920. *RUR and The Insect Play*, P Selver, trans, Oxford, OUP, 1961. ISBN 9780192810106.

Chaucer, Geoffrey, *The Canterbury Tales*. c1380-89. *The Riverside Chaucer*, ed Larry D Benson. Oxford, OUP, 1987. ISBN 9780395290316.

Christie, Agatha, *Murder on the Orient Express*. 1934. London, HarperCollins Publishers, 2007. ISBN 9780007119318.

Christie, Agatha, *And Then There Were None*. 1939 (as *Ten Little Niggers*). London, HarperCollins Publishers, 2011. ISBN 9780062073488.

Clarke, Arthur C, 'The Sentinel'. 1951. Clarke, Arthur C, *The Lost Worlds of 2001*. London, Sidgwick and Jackson Ltd, 1972. ISBN 9780283979040.

Coburn, Anthony, *The Masters of Luxor*. **Doctor Who: The Scripts**. London, Titan Books, 1992. ISBN 9781852683210.

Conan Doyle, Arthur, *The Valley of Fear*. 1914. Conan Doyle, Arthur, *The Penguin Complete Sherlock Holmes*. London, Penguin Books Ltd, 2009. ISBN 9780141040288.

Cornell, Paul, Martin Day and Keith Topping, *Doctor Who: The Discontinuity Guide*. London, Virgin Publishing, 1995. ISBN 9780426204428.

Coleridge, Samuel Taylor, 'The Rime of the Ancient Mariner'. Wordsworth, William, and Samuel Taylor Coleridge, *Lyrical Ballads*. London, J&A Arch, 1798.

Crompton, Richmal, *William's Television Show*. London, Macmillan Children's Books, 1958. ISBN 9780333555484.

Davies, Russell T, and Benjamin Cook, *The Writer's Tale: The Final Chapter*. London, BBC Books, 2010. ISBN 9781846078613.

De Burgh Miller, Jon, *Deus Le Volt*. **Time Hunter**. Tolworth, Telos Publishing Ltd, 2005. ISBN 9781903889497.

Dicks, Terrance. *Doctor Who and the Genesis Of The Daleks*. **The Target Doctor Who Library** #27. London, WH Allen, 1976. ISBN 9780426112600.

Dicks, Terrance, *Doctor Who and the Image Of The Fendahl*. **The Target Doctor Who Library** #34. London, WH Allen, 1979. ISBN 9780426200772.

Dicks, Terrance, *The Eight Doctors*. **Doctor Who: The Eighth Doctor Adventures**. London, BBC Books, 1997. ISBN 9780563405635.

Drabble, Margaret, *The Oxford Companion to English Literature*. Fifth edition. Oxford, Oxford University Press, 1995. ISBN 9780198614531.

Hale, Terry, ed, *Tales of the Dead: Ghost Stories of the Villa Diodati*. Basingstoke, The Gothic Society, 1992. ISBN I87441000309.

Heinlein, Robert, *Space Cadet*. 1948. Kindle edition. New York, Spectrum Literary Agency Inc, 2014. ASIN B00IKVE14M.

Hogan, James P, *Inherit the Stars*. New York, Del Rey Books, 1977. ISBN 9780345289070.

James, MR, *Ghost Stories of An Antiquary*. London, Edward Arnold, 1904.

Johns, Captain WE, *Return to Mars*. London, Hodder & Stoughton, 1955. ASIN B000X3XY70.

Johnson, Tom, *Hammer Films: An Exhaustive Filmography*. Kindle edition. Jefferson NC, McFarland & Co, 1995. ASIN B00GU1G1X8.

Joshi, ST, *Lovecraft and a World in Transition: Collected Essays*. Kindle edition. New York, Hippocampus Press, 2015. ASIN B00SU31OY0.

Leitch, Gillian I, ed, *Doctor Who in Time and Space: Essays on Themes, Characters, History and Fandom, 1963-2012*. **Critical**

Explorations in Science Fiction and Fantasy #39. Jefferson NC, McFarland & Co, 2013. ISBN 9780786465491.

Lewis, CS, *The CS Lewis Signature Classics Collection*. Kindle Edition. San Francisco, HarperCollins, 2012. ASIN B007XJ74EG.

Lewis, CS, *The Space Trilogy*. London, HarperCollins 2013. ISBN 9780007528417.

Ligotti, Thomas, *Songs of a Dead Dreamer*. 1986. Kindle edition. Burton MI, Subterranean Press, 2012. ASIN B00AAHR4C0.

Lovecraft, HP, *Selected Letters Volume 2*. Sauk City WI, Arkham House, 1968. ISBN 9780870540295.

Lovecraft, HP, *Letters to James F. Morton*. David E Schultz and ST Joshi, eds. New York, Hippocampus Press, 2011. ISBN 9780984480234

Lovecraft, HP, *The Necronomicon: The Best Weird Fiction of HP Lovecraft*. London, Gollancz, 2008. ISBN 9780575081567.

Lumley, Brian, *The Taint and Other Novellas*. Oxford, Solaris, 2008. ISBN 9781844165926.

Lumley, Brian, *The Caller of The Black*. Sauk City WI, Arkham House, 1971. ISBN 9780870540592.

Moorcock, Michael, *Warrior of Mars*. London, Hodder & Stoughton, 1986. ISBN 9780450058950.

Moore, Patrick, *Can You Speak Venusian? A Guide to the Independent Thinkers*. Devon, David & Charles Publishers Ltd, 1972. ISBN 9780715356913.

Moore, Patrick, and Garry Hunt, *The Atlas of the Solar System*. London, Artists House, 1990. ISBN 9780861341252.

Muir, John Kenneth, *A Critical History of Doctor Who on Television*. Jefferson NC, McFarland & Co, 2007. ISBN 9780786437160.

Neugebauer, O, *A History of Ancient Mathematical Astronomy* vol 1. London, Springer, 1976. ISBN 9780387901824.

Niven, Larry, *Flatlander: The Collected Tales of Gil Hamilton*. New York, Del Rey, 1995. ISBN 9780345394804.

The Compact Oxford English Dictionary. Second edition, 1991. ISBN 9780198612582.

O'Regan Gerald, *Giants of Computing: A Compendium of Select, Pivotal Pioneers*. London, Springer, 2013. ISBN 9781447153399.

Peacock, Thomas Love, *Nightmare Abbey*. London, T Hookham Jr, 1818.

Peake, Mervyn, *Titus Groan*. London, Eyre and Spottiswoode, 1946.

Peake, Mervyn, *Gormenghast*. London, Eyre and Spottiswoode, 1950.

Peake, Mervyn, *Titus Alone*. London, Eyre and Spottiswoode, 1959.

Poe, Edgar Allan, *The Narrative of Arthur Gordon Pym of Nantucket*. New York, Harper & Brothers, 1838.

Proctor, Richard A, *Myths and Marvels of Astronomy*. 1896. Kindle edition. ASIN B0082PMD96.

Reynolds, GWM, *Wagner, the Wehr-Wolf*. Serialised pamphlets, 1846-47. New York, Hurst & Co, 1847.

Rymer, James Malcolm and Thomas Peckett Prest, *Varney the Vampire*. Serialised pamphlets, 1845-47. London, E Lloyd, 1847.

Shelley, Mary, *Frankenstein, or The Modern Prometheus*. 1818 revised 1831. Oxford World's Classics 1818 text. Oxford, OUP, 1998. ISBN 9780192833662.

Sitchin, Zecharia, *The 12th Planet*. 1976. Kindle edition. ASIN B0057GR5ZA.

Sleight, Graham, *The Doctor's Monsters: Meanings of The Monstrous In Doctor Who*. New York, I. B. Tauris & Co Ltd, 2012. ISBN 9781848851788.

Smith, Anne Eliza, *Seola*. 1878. Kindle edition. San Francisco, Internet Archive, 2015. ASIN B00SI2H7QC.

Solomon, Dr Robert, *The Little Book of Mathematical Principles*. London, New Holland Publishers, 2008. ISBN 9781847730602.

Stableford, Brian, *The Walking Shadow: A Promethean Scientific Romance*. 1979. Rockville MD, Wildside Press, 2013. ISBN 9781299783058.

Stoker, Bram, *Dracula*. London, Archibald Constable & Co, 1897.

Sutherland, John, *Is Heathcliff a Murderer?* Oxford, OUP, 1996. ISBN 9780192825162.

Thompson, Ben, *Ban This Filth! Letters From the Mary Whitehouse Archive*. London, Faber and Faber, 2012. ISBN 9780571281497.

Thoren, Victor E, *The Lord of Uraniborg: A Biography of Tycho Brahe*. Cambridge, CUP, 1991. ISBN 9780521033077.

Tulloch, John, and Manuel Alvarado, *Doctor Who: The Unfolding Text*. New York, St Martin's Press, 1983. ISBN 9780333348482.

Turner, Alwyn, *Terry Nation: The Man Who Invented The Daleks*. London, Aurum Press, 2011. Kindle edition. ISBN 9781306483599.

Van Vogt, AE, *The Voyage of the Space Beagle*. London, Granada Publishing Ltd, 1959. ISBN 9780586024393.

Velikowsky, Immanuel, *Worlds in Collision*. London, Macmillan, 1950.

Walpole, Horace, *The Castle of Otranto*. 1764. London, The Folio Society, 1976. ISBN 9780850671032.

Periodicals

Doctor Who Magazine (DWM). Marvel UK, Panini, BBC, 1979-.

    'Doctor Who: The First 50 Years'. DWM #474, cover date July 2014.

    Barnes, Alan, 'The Fact of Fiction: Image of the Fendahl'. DWM #379, cover date February 2007.

Brackett, Leigh, 'Martian Quest'. *Astounding Science Fiction*, February 1940.

Chambers, JE and JJ Lissauer, 'A New Dynamical Model for the Lunar Late Heavy Bombardment', *Lunar and Planetary Science* #33, 2002.

Ellis, Warren, Karl Story and Chris Sprouse, **Ocean**. Wildstorm, 20014-05.

Moore, Alan, **The League of Extraordinary Gentlemen** volume 2. America's Best Comics, 2002-03.

Moore, Alan, JH Williams III and Mick Gray, **Promethea**. America's Best Comics, 1999-2005.

Moore, Alan, and Jacen Burrows, **Providence**. Avatar Press, 2015-.

Moore, Alan, and Steve Bissette, **1963**. Image Comics, 1993.

Morrison, Grant, and Chris Burnham, **Nameless**. Image, 2015.

Parkin, Lance, 'The Quatermass Irrelevancy', *Matrix* #51.

Radio Times. BBC Magazines, Immediate Media Company, 1923-.

Thomson, Helen, 'Death-Clock in Cells Counts Down to Cancer', *New Scientist*, 14 November 2015.

Wenz, John, 'According to Tajikistan, There's a New Fifth Planet From the Sun Called Tajikistan', *Popular Mechanics*, 2 September 2015.

Television

The Ascent of Man. BBC, Time-Life Films, 1973.

Beyond the Rave. Hammer Films, 2008.

Blake's 7. BBC, 1978-81.

> *Pressure Point*, 1979.
>
> *Gambit*, 1979.
>
> *Weapon*, 1979.
>
> *Voice from the Past*, 1979.

Doctor Who. BBC, 1963-.

> 'Life After Who – Philip Hinchcliffe'. *The Android Invasion* DVD release, 2012.

The Creature. BBC, 1955.

K-9 and Company. BBC, 1981.

> *A Girl's Best Friend*.

The Midsomer Murders (1997-)

> *Dance with the Dead* (2006)

Out of the Unknown. BBC, 1965-71.

> *The World in Silence*, 1966.

The Quatermass Experiment. BBC, 1953.

Quatermass II. BBC, 1955.

Quatermass and the Pit. BBC, 1958-59.

Norbert Smith: A Life. BBC, 1989.

The Stone Tape. BBC, 1972.

They Saved Hitler's Brain. Paragon Films Inc, Sans-S, 1968.

Thirty-Minute Theatre. BBC, 1965-73.

> *The Metal Martyr*, 1967.

Survivors. BBC, 1975-77.

Film

Baker, Roy Ward, dir, *Quatermass and the Pit*. Hammer Films, 1967.

Brabin, Charles, dir, *The Mask of Fu Manchu*. Cosmopolitan Productions, MGM, 1932.

Boorman, John, dir, *Zardoz*. John Boorman Productions, 1974.

Cahn, Edward L, dir, *It! The Terror From Beyond Space*. Robert E Kent Productions, 1958.

Cooper, Merian C, and Ernest B Schoedsack, dirs, *King Kong*. RKO Radio Pictures, 1933.

Coppola, Francis Ford, dir, *The Godfather*. Paramount Pictures, Alfran Productions, 1972.

Day, Robert, dir, *She*. Associated British Picture Corporation, Hammer Films, 1965.

Donner, Richard, dir, *Lethal Weapon*. Warner Bros, Silver Pictures, 1987.

Fisher, Terence, dir, *The Curse of Frankenstein*. Warner Bros, Hammer Films, 1957.

Fisher, Terence, dir, *The Devil Rides Out*. Associated British-Pathé, Hammer Films, Seven Arts Pictures, 1968.

Fleischer, Richard, dir, *Fantastic Voyage*. Twentieth Century Fox Film Corporation, 1956.

Florey, Robert, dir, *The Beast with Five Fingers*. Warner Bros, 1946.

Francis, Freddie, dir, *Dr Terror's House of Horrors*. Amicus Productions, 1965.

Francis, Freddie, dir, *The Skull*. Amicus Productions, 1965.

      Newman, Kim. Interview on *The Skull* DVD release, 2015.

Frankenheimer, John, dir, *The Manchurian Candidate*. MC Productions, 1962.

Freund, Karl, dir, *The Mummy*. Universal Pictures, 1932.

Guest, Val, dir, *The Quatermass Xperiment*. Exclusive Films, Hammer Films, 1955.

Guest, Val, dir, *Quatermass 2*. Hammer Films, 1957.

Guest, Val, dir, *The Abominable Snowman*. Clarion Films, Hammer Films, 1957.

Hamilton, Guy, dir, *Live and Let Die*. Eon Films, 1973.

Hill, George Roy, dir, *Thoroughly Modern Millie*. Universal Pictures, Ross Hunter Productions, 1967.

Kubrick, Stanley, dir, *2001: A Space Odyssey*. MGM, Stanley Kubrick Productions, 1968.

Lourie, Eugene, dir, *Gorgo*. King Brothers Productions, 1961.

Lucas, George, dir, *Star Wars*. Lucasfilm, Twentieth Century Fox Film Corporation, 1977.

Mamoulian, Rouben, dir, *Dr Jekyll and Mr Hyde*. Paramount Pictures, 1931.

Moore, Alan, *Ragnarok*. Nutland Video, 1982.

Mueller, Karl, dir, *Mr Jones*. Campfire, Preferred Content, Preferred Film & TV, 2013.

Murnau, FW, dir, *Nosferatu*. Jofa-Atelier Berlin-Johannisthal, Prana-Film GmbH, 1922.

Norman, Leslie, dir, *X the Unknown*. Exclusive Films, Hammer Films, 1956.

Nyby, Christian, dir, *The Thing from Another World*. RKO Radio Pictures, Winchester Pictures Corporation,1951.

Pogue, John, dir, *The Quiet Ones*. Exclusive Media Group, Hammer Films, Traveling Picture Show Company, 2014.

Polanski, Roman, dir, *Rosemary's Baby*. William Castle Productions, 1968.

Reitherman, Wolfgang, dir, *Robin Hood*. Walt Disney Productions, 1973.

Scott, Ridley, dir, *Alien*. Brandywine Productions, Twentieth Century-Fox, 1979.

Siegel, Don, dir, *Invasion of the Body Snatchers*. Walter Wanger Productions, 1956.

Whale, James, dir, *Frankenstein*. Universal Pictures, 1931.

Wiene, Robert, dir, *The Cabinet of Dr Caligari* (*Das Cabinet des Dr Caligary*). Decla-Bioscop AG, 1920.

Wilcox, Fred McLeod, dir, *Forbidden Planet*. MGM, 1956.

Yeaworth Jr, Irvin S, dir, *The Blob*. Fairview Productions, Tonylyn Productions Inc, Valley Forge Films, 1958.

Audio CD

Kaldor City. Magic Bullet Productions, 2001-04.

Richards, Justin. *The Inquiry*. **Gallifrey**. Big Finish Productions, 2004.

Web

'Ancestry'. www.ancestry.co.uk. Accessed 22 February 2016.

BBC Genome Project. http://genome.ch.bbc.co.uk/. Accessed 22 February 2016.

'Brian W Aldiss on "Frankenstein"'. *Vulpes Libris*, 4 December 2008. https://vulpeslibris.wordpress.com/2008/12/04/brian-w-aldiss/. Accessed 22 February 2016.

'Distances between the Planets'. *Planets.org.uk.* http://www.planetsedu.com/distances-between-the-planets/. Accessed 22 February 2016.

'The Dwarf Planet Ceres'. *Astronomical Adventures.* www.astrodigital.org/astronomy/ceres.html. Accessed 22 February 2016.

'Doctor Who Appreciation Society 1977 Convention'. http://www.richardwho.com/conventions/dwas1977/index.asp. Accessed 22 February 2016.

'Find My Past'. www.findmypast.com. Accessed 22 February 2016.

'Graham Williams (1980s)'. https://drwhointerviews.wordpress.com/2009/10/25/graham-williams-1980s/. Accessed 22 February 2016.

'One of our Planets Is Missing'. *The Galaxy Express.* http://www.thegalaxyexpress.com/one-our-planets-missing. Accessed 22 February 2016.

'Return to Mars'. *www.wejohns.com.* http://www.wejohns.com/SciFi/02%20Return%20to%20Mars/. Accessed 22 February 2016.

'Wilhelm Olbers'. *Encyclopaedia Britannica.* http://www.britannica.com/biography/Wilhelm-Olbers. Accessed 22 February 2016.

Browning, Richard, 'Historic inflation calculator: how the value of money has changed since 1900'. *This Is Money.* http://www.thisismoney.co.uk/money/bills/article-1633409/Historic-inflation-calculator-value-money-changed-1900.html. Accessed 22 February 2016.

Doctorow, Cory, 'Alan Moore on Lovecraft and the 20th Century'. *BoingBoing*, 3 November 2015. http://boingboing.net/2015/11/03/alan-moore-on-lovecraft-and-th.html. Accessed 22 February 2016.

Koberlein, Brian, 'Astronomers find New Object, Possible Super-Earth in Our Solar System'. https://briankoberlein.com/2015/12/18/astronomers-find-new-object-possible-super-earth-in-our-solar-system/. Accessed 22 February 2016.

Major, Jason, 'How Many Asteroids are Out There?' *Universe Today*, 25 September 2012. http://www.universetoday.com/97571/how-many-asteroids-are-out-there/. Accessed 22 February 2016.

Mulkern, Patrick. 'Doctor Who Story Guide: Image of the Fendahl'. http://www.radiotimes.com/blog/2010-10-21/image-of-the-fendahl. Accessed 22 February 2016.

Stevens, Alan, 'Image of the Fendahl'. http://www.kaldorcity.com/features/antecedents/fendahl.html. Accessed 22 February 2016.

BIOGRAPHY

Simon Bucher-Jones is the author (or co-author) of six novels, several short stories, a cursed play, and at least 161 poems.

With Mark Clapham he co-authored *The Taking of Planet 5,* a **Doctor Who** book involving no actual appearance by the Fendahl, despite what the Wikipedia page for the TV story says.

He has a BA (Hon) in English Literature from Sheffield, and has watched more B-movies and old science fiction films than is generally considered advisable. His interest in astronomy and science fact and fiction, dates back as far as he can remember. HP Lovecraft has been one of his favourite writers since he reached 'L' in the library.

He turned 13 the month before *Image of the Fendahl* was shown for the first time on the BBC. It's one of his favourite **Doctor Who** stories – you may have noticed.